BEGINNINGS, MIDDLES, & ENDS

BEGINNINGS, MIDDLES, *&* ENDS

WRITER'S DIGEST
BOOKS

WritersDigest.*com*
Cincinnati, Ohio

NANCY KRESS

For more resources for writers, visit www.writersdigest.com/books.

To receive a free weekly e-mail newsletter delivering tips and updates about writing and about Writer's Digest products, register directly at http://newsletters.fwpublications.com.

20 19 18 17   10 9 8 7 6

Distributed in Canada by Fraser Direct
100 Armstrong Avenue
Georgetown, Ontario, Canada L7G 5S4
Tel: (905) 877-4411

Distributed in the U.K. and Europe by F+W Media International
Brunel House, Newton Abbot, Devon, TQ12 4PU, England
Tel: (+44) 1626-323200, Fax: (+44) 1626-323319
E-mail: postmaster@davidandcharles.co.uk

Distributed in Australia by Capricorn Link
P.O. Box 704, Windsor, NSW 2756 Australia
Tel: (02) 4577-3555

Edited by: Jack Heffron and Melissa Wuske
Designed by: Claudean Wheeler
Illustrations © Dover Pictura/Art Nouveau
Production coordinated by: Debbie Thomas

DEDICATION

For Miriam, Nick, Mark, and all the other writers I've been privileged to work with as students

ABOUT THE AUTHOR

Nancy Kress is the author of twenty-eight books: three about writing and the rest, fiction of various genres. Her work has garnered her four Nebula Awards and two Hugo Awards. For sixteen years she was the fiction columnist for *Writer's Digest* magazine, and now frequently teaches writing at various venues around the country. Nancy lives in Seattle with writer Jack Skillingstead and Cosette, the world's most spoiled toy poodle.

CONTENTS

"A writer's problem does not change. He himself changes and the world he lives in changes but his problem remains the same. It is always how to write truly and having found what is true, to project it in such a way that it becomes part of the experience of the person who reads it."

—ERNEST HEMINGWAY

INTRODUCTION
THE STORY IN YOUR HEAD

There's a story in your head—or maybe just the start of a story. Characters are walking around in there, talking to each other, doing things to the furniture, gesturing and shouting and laughing. You can see it all so clearly, like a movie rolling in your mind. It's going to be terrific. Excited, you sit down to write.

But something happens. The story that comes out on the page isn't the same as the story in your head. The dialogue is flatter, the action doesn't read right, the *feel* just isn't the same. There's a gap between the story you can visualize and the one you know how to write. And at the moment, that gap resembles the Mariana Trench—deep, scary, and uncrossable.

If you've ever felt this way about your writing, you're not alone. The truth is that there's *always* a gap between the story as you imagined it—compelling, insightful, rich with subtle nuance—and what actually ends up in the manuscript. This is because stories must be written, and read, one word at a time, with information accumulating in the reader's mind to create the full picture. This slow, linear accretion of impressions can't ever quite equal that perfect flash of inspiration in which all the parts of the story—action, meaning, nuances, insights—burst into the brain all at once. Words, unlike movies, are not a multisensory event. Words are symbols, and symbols don't work directly on the human senses. They work secondhand, through suggestions to the reader's imagination, through words describing what you saw in *your* imagination.

No wonder there's always a gap between the story in the writer's head and the one she puts into the reader's head.

For professional writers, that gap may be small. A professional learns what information to present—and in what order—to make the words convey her original vision as closely as possible. The beginning writer must learn this, too. One way to do that is to write a lot—some people say a million words—until you get better through trial and error. Another is to receive reliable criticism on which parts of your story are conveying your vision and which are not. A good writing class can do this for you. A third way is to read books like this to learn how good writers present information to their reader's imagination.

That "third way" isn't really sufficient by itself, of course. Learning *about* writing won't help you write better unless you actually apply what you learn to a story in progress—just as learning about the ideal golf swing won't improve your score unless you actually practice on the links. There's no substitute for practice. The Mariana Trench doesn't get crossed by discussing it.

Nor will this book help you improve the quality of the story in your head. That vision comes from everything about you: your experiences, your imagination, your beliefs about the world, your powers of perception, your interests, your sophistication, your previous reading, your soul. Vision, sometimes called talent, is not a teachable attribute.

What *is* teachable, and what this book can help you with, is craft. Craft is the process of getting the story in your head onto the page in a form that readers can follow, and remain interested in, and enjoy. Finding that form means making literally hundreds of decisions in the course of a short story: What do I show first? How much background should I tell here? What scene should I put next? This plot development or that one?

This noun or that one? This ending or something else I haven't thought of yet? Help!

Craft can be helped. Craft can be taught. Craft can help you narrow—if not completely eliminate—the gap between the story in your head and the story on the page. Craft is a set of navigation tools for crossing the Mariana Trench.

THREE PATTERNS FOR STORIES THAT AREN'T WORKING

In my years of teaching, I've noticed three distinct patterns in student stories, which are often also habitual patterns for the stories' writers. One kind of story starts very slowly. Events drag, characters seem confused, and even the prose is a bit clumsy. Then, somewhere around page five for a short story or chapter three for a novel, the writer suddenly hits his stride or finds his voice. The story picks up, and from that point on it becomes more and more interesting.

This writer needs help with beginnings.

A second type of story starts well, with a strong hook and a sure tone. The first scene presents intriguing characters and raises interesting questions. Sometimes even the second scene works well. After that, however, the story flounders. It's as if the writer didn't know how to answer the intriguing questions or develop the characters and their situation. In desperation he plunges ahead anyway, and the story winds down into confusion or dragginess or boredom.

This writer needs help with middles.

Finally, there is the story that sustains interest right to the last scene. The reader is racing along, dying to know how it all comes out or what it all means. But she never does. Instead she finds a resolution that leaves major plotlines hanging, or is out of character, or doesn't seem to add up to anything meaningful, or trails off into pseudosymbolism that doesn't seem connected to the events of the story. The reader feels cheated. The writer gets rejected—but often not right away. Many such stories earn editorial requests for a rewrite, since the editor doesn't want to believe that such promising fireworks have to fizzle out. The request spotlights the problem but doesn't solve it. This writer needs help with endings.

To some extent, of course, these are artificial divisions. What you write in the beginning of your story is intimately connected with the middle, which in turn gives birth to the end. A well-written story is a living whole. But by examining beginnings, middles, and ends one at a time, we can identify some of the problems associated with each. By looking at solutions, we can address some of the issues of craft that move a story from the writer's head to the page.

Even the Mariana Trench, after all, has been conquered. On January 23,1960, the bathyscaphe Trieste settled 35,800 feet below the surface of the Pacific, shining light for the first time on the murky depths of the Trench.

Bon voyage!

PART ONE
Beginnings

·····················

CHAPTER 1

THE VERY BEGINNING: YOUR OPENING SCENE

You are an editor. You have in front of you a large pile of unsolicited short stories, or an even larger pile of first novels. You also have an editorial meeting in two hours, three phone calls to return this morning, and a problem with the art department that you wish would go away by itself but which probably won't. You pick up the first manuscript in the pile and start reading it. How far do you get before you decide to finish it or to put it back in its self-addressed stamped envelope with a form rejection slip?

Before we answer that question, let's look at the other end of this fictional communication. That's you, the writer of this story. You've worked hard on it. You have hopes for it—if not fame and fortune (at least, not right off), then certainly publication. This manuscript is important to you. In an ideal world, the editor would give this story the same attention you did, reading it without distraction (perhaps sitting in a wing chair in a cozy, book-lined study), with care, all the way through.

But this is not an ideal world. The truth is, you have about three paragraphs in a short story, three pages in a novel, to capture that editor's attention enough for her to finish your story. With busy editors, the biblical prophecy is, alas, too often true: "The first shall be last."

Does this discourage you? It shouldn't. It's just a fact of literary life, like overdue royalty statements and inept reviewers. And unlike those regrettable phenomena, this can work to your advantage. Once you know that you have just three paragraphs to create a good first impression, you can spend your time rewriting and polishing that opening until it convinces an editor to keep reading.

You can deliberately incorporate the qualities that make an opening interesting and original: character, conflict, specificity, and credibility. These are, of course, elements that are present throughout the entire length of successful stories and novels. However, for beginnings they have particular applications and forms. But before we consider these four elements, we must consider something even more basic to the success of any story's beginning—and its middle and its end. This crucial concept is the implicit promise.

THE IMPLICIT PROMISE: FRAMEWORK FOR THE WHOLE

Every story makes a promise to the reader. Actually, two promises, one emotional and one intellectual, since the function of stories is to make us both feel and think.

The emotional promise goes: *Read this and you'll be entertained, or thrilled, or scared, or titillated, or saddened, or nostalgic, or uplifted—but always absorbed.*

There are three versions of the intellectual promise. The story can promise (1) *Read this and you'll see this world from a different perspective;* (2) *Read this and you'll have confirmed what you already want to believe about this world;* or (3) *Read this and you'll learn of a different, more interesting world than this.* The last promise, it should be noted, can exist on its own or coexist with either of the first two.

Thus, a romance promises to entertain and titillate us, to confirm our belief that "Love can conquer all," and to transport us to a more glamorous world than this one, where the heroine (and by vicarious identification, the reader) is beautiful, well-dressed, and ultimately beloved. A mystery novel promises an entertaining intellectual challenge (Whodunit?), confirmation that the human mind can understand events, the satisfaction of justice, and—sometimes—insights into how human nature operates under pressure. A literary novel such as Toni Morrison's *Beloved,* about slavery and its aftermath, delivers emotions of anger, horror, guilt, or recoil—not pleasant emotions, but strong ones. Intellectually it may unsettle our view of the world. "Real art," writes critic Susan Sontag, "has the capacity to make us nervous."

As a writer, you must know what promise your story or novel makes. Your reader will know. She may buy your book because it belongs to a genre that promises certain things (romance, science fiction, horror, political thriller). Or she may come to your story without preconceptions, in which case she'll form them pretty quickly from your characters, tone, plot, and style.

By the time she's read your opening, your reader knows what you've implicitly promised. A satisfying middle is one that develops that promise with specificity and interest. A satisfying ending is one that delivers on the promise, providing new insight or comfortable confirmation or vicarious happiness. Even when it's surprising in some way, the ending feels inevitable, because it fulfills the promise of the story. And—this is important—the ending feels satisfying only because the beginning set up the implicit promise in the first place.

Consider an example, Daniel Reyes's much-anthologized story "Flowers for Algernon," which was made into the movie Charley. "Flowers For Algernon" is about Charlie Gordon (the transition from page to screen apparently affects spelling), a retarded adult who is the butt of cruel jokes by his coworkers at a bakery. Charlie undergoes an untested operation to radically raise his I.Q. The story is told through Charlie's diary entries. They start out short, misspelled, and simple, and become increasingly complex as Charlie surpasses in intellectual ability all the doctors conducting the experiment. Charlie's relationships with them, with coworkers and with women change drastically— although not necessarily for the better.

From the beginning, Charlie is portrayed as likable; the world is portrayed as logical if not always kind; injustice is inherent in Charlie's initial situation—why should somebody so good be treated so badly? The promise is made that whatever happens to Charlie, it will follow the laws of science, will keep us on his side, and may not be fair, since the universe isn't fair. The middle of the story elaborates on these conditions, pitting Charlie's intense desire to be smarter against our society's distrust of the man who "gets above himself." The ending fulfills the promise. The effects of the operation turn out to be only temporary. Charlie slides back down the I.Q. scale; he has trouble even remembering what happened to him; he's once more at the bottom of the social heap but kept from unhappiness by his own indomitable, sweet nature. The ending delivers on the promise of the first two-thirds of the story.

Suppose, however, that Keyes had ended the story differently. Suppose Charlie had been hit by a bus and killed. Or suppose he had become a killer himself, enraged by all the injustices done him, and the story had turned into a bloodbath. Or suppose the operation had been permanent and Charlie had become as arrogant and unfeeling as the doctors. Or suppose the operation had been permanent and Charlie ended up happy.

None of these endings would have been satisfying. Being hit by a bus, a random death, wouldn't have delivered on the promise of logic implied by all the science. Charlie's becoming either a killer or a bastard wouldn't have delivered on the implicit promise that here was somebody we can like, somebody to root for. The happy ending wouldn't have delivered on the injustices of the world so carefully set up in the early scenes of a good man victimized by circumstances.

Note that this analysis implies that you must know from the beginning what implicit promise your story makes. Actually, this is both true and not true. The final draft must contain the same promise to the reader throughout, with the promise made in the beginning, developed in the middle, and fulfilled at the end. But writing a story isn't as mechanical as building a house. There are no blueprints. Sometimes a writer doesn't know what promise she's really making until it emerges sometime during the first draft. That's all right. We'll explore the development of the implicit promise, and its implications for revision, throughout this book. What's important to remember as you write your beginning is that you are making a promise to the reader, even though at this point you may not be sure just what it is.

In your first scene, however, your main goal is to keep your reader interested. You do that through focusing not on overall meaning but on the four elements that make a first scene compelling: character, conflict, specificity, and credibility.

CHARACTER: WHO GOES THERE?

Your opening should give the reader a person to focus on. In a short story, this person should turn up almost immediately; he should be integral to the story's main action; he should be an individual, not just a type. In a novel, the main character may take longer to appear: Anna Karenina doesn't show up in her own novel until chapter eighteen. However, somebody interesting should appear very early. In Anna Karenina, it's Anna's brother Stepan, who is both integral to the plot and very much an individual.

To see how these goals can be accomplished in a very short space, consider the opening of Raymond Carver's six-page story "Fat":

> I am sitting over coffee and cigarettes at my friend Rita's and
> I am telling her about it.

> Here is what I tell her.
>
> It is late of a slow Wednesday when Herb seats the fat
> man at my station.
>
> This fat man is the fattest person I have ever seen, though
> he is neat-appearing and well-dressed enough. Everything
> about him is big. But it is the fingers I remember best. When
> I stop at the table next to his to see to the old couple, I first
> notice the fingers.

Here, immediately, is a character for the reader to focus on. Actually, two people, but let's discuss the narrator. She's not even talking about herself, yet she emerges not as an abstract job description ("waitress") but as an individual. This person is observant ("I first notice the fingers"). She is reflective; she has obviously given some thought to the incident she's about to relate to Rita. Her speech is simple and repetitive (" … and I am telling her about it. Here is what I tell her"), suggesting not only a definite socioeconomic class but also a certain kind of mind: one that can consider a small incident meaningful enough to emphasize, meaningful enough to weigh, eventually meaningful enough to be changed by. All of this is hinted at subtly; most readers will not stop to analyze the character at this point. But readers will sense that there is a character here, a genuine person.

Contrast Carver's opening with the character in the following unsuccessful beginning:

> The fall day was hot. Ted Henderson drove to the school
> and parked the car. He wore a dark blue suit, black shoes,
> and the maroon tie Kathy had given him for Christmas. He
> climbed the steps and opened the door. Inside, it was cooler.
> The school office told him Mrs. Kelly would join him soon.
> Ted sat down to wait.
>
> When Mrs. Kelly arrived, she led him into a conference
> room. They sat down.

"I'd like to discuss my daughter Jane's grades," Ted said. "Her report card wasn't very good."

This opening has exactly the same number of words as Carver's (91), but what have we learned about Ted Henderson? That he wears a suit, that someone named Kathy once gave him a tie for Christmas, that he has a daughter named Jane who isn't doing well in school, and that he has gone to visit Jane's teacher.

But what kind of person is this Ted? Is he conferring with Mrs. Kelly because he's worried about Jane? Or angry at her for doing badly? Or angry at Mrs. Kelly for not doing a better job as a teacher? Does he feel that Jane's poor performance reflects on him?

Is he hoping the whole thing can be taken care of quickly because he has an important corporate meeting at eleven o'clock? Or has he carefully asked his boss for the whole day off so he can schedule the conference at the convenience of the teacher, an educated woman who makes him nervous? Is that dark blue suit his only one, a little shiny in the seat and usually worn just for church? Or is it expensive English wool, conservatively tailored? Or maybe it's a sporty-looking Italian silk, the tie knotted only loosely, the trousers breaking at exactly the right place over leather loafers.

The point is, we haven't a clue about Ted Henderson's personality. It's possible that the writer will individualize him more as the story goes on—but we probably won't read long enough to find out.

Most successful openings give the reader a genuine character because most stories are about human beings. A few, however, are actually about something else. Shirley Jackson's "The Lottery," for instance, begins with several paragraphs about villagers gathering for an annual lottery. None of the villagers are individualized much. Few are even given names. The equipment used for the lottery is described in much more detail than the people. That is because in this story, the lottery itself is the main character, with a life and force of its own—which is the whole point.

Similarly, some novels delay the entrance of a genuine character until chapter two, when something else has enough force to substitute. John Steinbeck's *The Grapes of Wrath* devotes chapter one to a detailed description of the devastation done by drought to the Oklahoma Dust Bowl. It works because this dry desolation becomes both motivator and symbol for the entire novel. Such structuring, however, is rare, and you will probably be better off getting people on your novelistic stage as quickly as possible.

CONFLICT: COMING SOON TO A SCENE NEAR YOU

The point to remember about conflict is that it arises because something is not going as expected. Your readers should suspect that as early as your first few paragraphs.

Calling for conflict in the opening few paragraphs of a story doesn't mean that your first sentence must feature a body hurtling past a sixth-story window (although it might). Some stories and novels feature overt, dramatic conflict: character versus character (as in thrillers, where one country's spy is pitted against another's), character versus nature (consider James Dickey's action-laden *Deliverance*), or character versus society (Shirley Jackson's "The Lottery," which ends with a stoning). In other stories, however, the conflict will be smaller in scale: family strife, romantic misunderstandings, personal economic gain or loss. The conflict may even be so subtle it exists solely inside the skull of one character, with the others not even aware of his anxiety or distress. But no matter what kind of conflict your story explores, its nature should be hinted at in your opening, even though the development of the conflict won't occur until later.

Look again, for example, at the opening of the Carver story "Fat." The hint of conflict is very subtle, but it is there: in the narrator's determination to tell the story to Rita, in the fact that she considers waiting on such a huge person to be out of the ordinary, in the fact that both writer and reader know that in our society weight is an emotional issue. All these clues will be developed into greater conflict throughout the story—and all are implied in the effective opening.

Often a short story hints at conflict as early as the first line. Following are the first lines from four different stories, which happen to be the first four stories in an anthology I pulled at random off my shelves. Every one promises conflict:

> "Off there to the right—somewhere—is a large island," said Whitney. "It's rather a mystery—"
> —Richard Connell, "The Most Dangerous Game"

(Why is the island mysterious? What's being hidden?)

> It was the eve of August Bank Holiday that the latest recruit became the leader of the Wormsley Common Gang.
> —Graham Greene, "The Destructors"

(An inversion of the natural social order, in which a new recruit would have the lowest standing, not the highest. Promises social problems.)

> As Mr. Nilson, well known in the City, opened the window of his dressing room on Campden Hill, he experienced a peculiar sweetish sensation in the back of his throat, and a feeling of emptiness just under his left rib.
> —John Galsworthy, "The Japanese Quince"

(Feelings that are both peculiar and empty promise anxiety, which in turn leads to conflict.)

> It was a hard jolt for me, one of the most bitterest I ever had to face.
> —Sherwood Anderson, "I'm a Fool"

(An obvious problem—how will he face this bitter jolt—and just what is it?)

What about novels? Here you have a little longer to introduce conflict. Even so, many novels do so on the first page. Such otherwise diverse writers as Leo Tolstoy *(Anna Karenina)*, Tom Wolfe (*Bonfire of the Vanities*), Anne Tyler *(Breathing Lessons)*, Danielle Steel *(Full Circle)* and Ken Follett *(The Key to Rebecca)* all show some endeavor going wrong by the end of page one (respectively: an extramarital affair, a political rally, a trip to a funeral, newlywed bliss, and a trek across the Sahara).

What works for this eclectic group of writers will work for you, too. Begin with an indication—subtle or overt—that something is not going as expected, or someone is experiencing disturbing emotions, or something is about to change.

SPECIFICITY: THAT'S A NEW ONE ON ME

Effective beginnings make use of specific details. These may be details of speech, setting, characters' thoughts—anything relevant. Effective use of details, more than any other single factor, distinguishes publishable manuscripts from those that have a good story line but somehow "aren't quite right for us." The right details gain you, the writer, three advantages:

- *Details anchor your story in concrete reality.* Not "Mary was an animal lover" but "Every night Mary fed her eighty-pound Labrador retriever all the best parts of what should have been John's T-bone." A specific animal, a specific time of day, a specific action to show us—not tell us—that Mary loves animals (maybe more than she loves John).

- *Details set your opening apart from the hundreds of others similar to it.* In the first paragraph, you haven't yet had time to develop subtleties of character or nuances of plot. Your story opens, say, at the dining room table—and so did ten others the editor saw this month. But yours will stand apart if the details you include are not the same ones the other ten authors used—in other words, not the first details to come to mind when you think of a generic dining room. These details are fresh, original, individual without being bizarre. They reveal that the writer has a fresh and meticulous eye. They pique interest by not being more of the same old thing.

- *Details convince the editor you know what you're talking about.* My story "Out of All Them Bright Stars," which takes place in a diner, begins, "So I'm filling the catsup bottles at the end of the night, and I'm listening to the radio Charlie has stuck up on top of a movable panel in the ceiling …" These two details came from my own experience as a diner waitress. When your details are accurate like this, the editor unconsciously awards you the precious prize of credibility. You sound like someone who knows about diners, so maybe you know how to tell a diner story as well. The editor reads on to find out.

Conversely, the wrong specific details can destroy your credibility in the first paragraph. I'll never forget the student whose story announced that "The blond trucker had just finished filling his diesel semi with regular when I drove up to the pump."

CREDIBILITY: CAN THIS PROSE BE TRUSTED?

Even the most accurate and interesting details, however, will be undermined if your prose itself lacks credibility. "Credibility" in this context is not easy to define. It's related to trust: Credible prose convinces the reader that the writer can handle the English language. He can be trusted. That sense of trust helps the reader suspend disbelief and enter into the world of the story. *If this guy can write prose this smooth,* goes the articulated-or-not reasoning, *it's worth seeing whether he can also*

tell a good story, or raise interesting questions, or make me think and feel
something beyond my usual experiences. I'll read on.

Credible prose is not, by itself, enough to make a story succeed; every editor sees plenty of manuscripts that are written smoothly but are dull or confusing or clichéd or implausible. The *lack* of credible prose, however, can be fatal. I know of one young novelist whose manuscript was initially rejected by an editor who told him that the story was exciting and the characters appealing, but the prose was so clumsy that the frustrated editor had scrawled "NO!" across entire paragraphs. (The author eventually rewrote it.)

"But," I hear you say, "if credible prose is so important, why do I see so many books—some of them bestsellers—with what I consider truly dreadful writing?" Good question. The answer is that those books sold on something other than the merits of their prose: a strong story, or the author's reputation, or characters that appeal to the readers of a well-defined genre. But whatever else those books have or don't have, credible prose can't hurt yours, especially if you're a beginning writer competing with established pros for an editor's attention. Writing well may not, alas, always be necessary, but it's always an asset. And the place to establish that you can write well is in your opening, while the editor is still giving you a chance.

What constitutes credible prose? It's more than just making sure subjects agree with verbs and modifiers don't dangle, although such concerns are a part of it. The essence of credibility is control. Credible prose reveals that you are in control of your words, sentences, and paragraphs. Specifically, you can control the following aspects of your writing.

Diction

Words are not misused. The credible author knows the difference between *unaffected* and *uneffected*, between *illusion* and *allusion*, and doesn't substitute one for the other. (One student irrevocably destroyed the serious tension of his war story by writing, "The commander had a firm but genital hold on his men.") Credible diction also avoids clichés. No one in a credible opening is fresh as a daisy, hungry as a bear, or quiet as a mouse—unless, of course, you are writing in first person and your character would use such clichés. Even then, make sure we can tell this is the character's voice, not the author's.

Economy

Credible prose uses only as many words as it needs to create its effects. It doesn't sprawl.

That doesn't mean, of course, that it can't be repetitious. Repetition can be used to great effect—if it's deliberately used to create a mood, an atmosphere, or a state of mind. Here's William Faulkner, the Great Repeater himself, describing Quentin Compson listening to Miss Rosa Coldfield in *Absalom, Absalom!*:

> Her voice would not cease, it would just vanish. There would be the dim coffin-smelling gloom sweet and over-sweet with the twice-bloomed wistaria against the outer wall by the savage quiet September sun impacted distilled and hyperdistilled ...

This is obviously very repetitive: of ceasing versus vanishing, of sweetness, of dimness *and* gloom, of sunlight that is impacted *and* distilled *and* hyperdistilled. But Faulkner is in complete control of his redundancy, using it relentlessly to paint a society obsessive about the past, a society repeating and repeating old sins, nurturing them by dwelling on them as long as possible (it will be three hours before Miss Coldfield tells Quentin what he's been summoned for). Repetitive prose is well suited to obsession and to dwelling on old sins. Nothing about Faulkner's redundancy feels accidental.

For most stories, however, economical prose will serve you much better. English poet Robert Southey said, "Be brief; for it is with words

as with sunbeams, the more they are condensed the deeper they burn."
One hundred fifty years later, this is still good advice, unfortunately un-
heeded by the author of the following sentence:

> He looked around the sparsely furnished main room, spar-
> tan in decor, boasting only a dilapidated couch, a sawed-off
> bench, a crusty sofa, plus a few other knickknacks strewn
> about the otherwise bare and dusty floor. It seemed to him
> a hopeless and depressing dump.

This prose sprawls. It takes forty-four words to say what could have been
said in twenty-two with no loss of information or effect. ("He studied
the Spartan main room: dilapidated couch, sawed-off bench, crusty sofa,
knickknacks on the dusty floor. *What a dump*, he thought.") Over the
course of a novel, that economy would cut the page count *in half*. If your
story can be told in half as many words, why should the reader have to
read twice as many? If an editor suspects that you, the writer, don't know
how to write economically, you lose credibility. To avoid that, scrutinize
your opening with a ruthless eye. Take out all repetitions that don't serve
a definite purpose.

Sentence Construction

Your natural style may lean toward short, crisp sentences or long, complex ones. Both are fine if they avoid awkwardness, a particular danger
of longer sentences. An awkward sentence is hard to read, is ambiguous,
or orders its clauses in a way that creates an impression different from
what was intended. These are all awkward sentences:

- He called his sister, Delia, in London and told her about the funeral for only eighty cents. (The sentence is made ludicrous by
  a misplaced modifier.)

- The flower bed, which the gardener, who had worked for the
  Smiths since 1944, had designed to hold roses but now held ba-

by's breath, Anna's favorite flower, needed weeding. (The sentence is confusing because it's interrupted by too many subsidiary phrases.)

- Bob wanted to swim, go sailing, and a lobster. (The sentence violates parallel structure.)

- He knew she was a criminal when he married her, which he did at a small church beloved by his mother, who had had the sole raising of him and done the best she could under difficult circumstances. (The sentence seems to start out about one thing and wanders to an entirely different point.)

This isn't a book about style; if you have trouble with sentence construction, find a book that is, and study it carefully. The point here is that awkward sentences will undermine your credibility, especially in your opening.

Sentence Variety

Since too many successive sentences of the same length can sound sing-song, credible prose varies sentence length. Again, this is a matter of having control of the effect you want to create. A short sentence following a series of long ones will have punch and drama; make sure the sentence therefore is *about* something punchy. A long sentence following a series of short ones will require heightened attention from the reader; make sure the content is worth it.

This paragraph, the opening of Steven Popkes's "The Egg," makes good use of sentence variety. It includes simple, compound, and complex sentences, of many different lengths:

> The rusty, pitted steel was soft but sharp as a knife. It was thirty or forty feet back to the beach. I didn't really want to climb back down; I didn't even have to look to convince myself. I knew how far it was. I tried rehearsing things I could say

> to my Aunt Sara: "Once I got that high, I had to keep going. It was too far to get back down" or "I was just trying to go up a little ways, but I got stuck." I shook my head. Didn't wash. She'd never *told* me not to come here …

The following paragraph, on the other hand, offers no variety in either sentence type (they're all compound) or sentence length:

> It was nearly twelve o'clock and I was getting tired. I wanted to leave, but John was still playing pinball. I tugged on his sleeve, and he scowled at me. It was always like this; we did what *he* wanted.

The effect is monotonous and tiring.

Parts of Speech

Finally, credible prose is not overloaded with adjectives and adverbs. Again, there are exceptions (look again at the brief passage from Faulkner). But, in general, excess modifiers are the mark of the amateur, and most stories improve when adjectives and adverbs are held to a minimum and strong verbs and nouns used instead. "He stumbled into his Corvette" is better than "He jerkily got into his sporty little car." Similarly, " 'Get out!' she shouted" is stronger than " 'I want you to leave,' she said angrily." If the dialogue is angry, we don't need the adverb.

Tone

Whatever the tone of your story—comic, serious, reportorial, ironic—the credible writer doesn't allow it to become self-indulgent. The focus should be on the story, not on the writer. This means resisting the impulse to overwrite through clever asides, through telling how important this all is (as opposed to showing us), through language too grandiose for the situation, through throwing in pointless foreign words or "in" slang, or through insistent punctuation ("Then the car slammed into the wall!!") If you make your story as straightforward as you can, keeping yourself out of it, the work will almost always be better for it. Let the story shine, not your devices for telling it.

Does all this sound daunting? It shouldn't. Probably you already have control of some of these aspects of credible prose. The rest you can strengthen when you rewrite and polish your opening. Many writers—I'm one of them—don't think about aspects of credible prose at all in the first draft. I concentrate on the story the first time through, revisions to the story the second time through, and prose quality in the third draft. It doesn't matter when you address the prose quality of your opening, so long as you *do*. When editors see credible prose, they become much more willing to put themselves in your hands for the rest of your story. Like a contractor who uses quality materials, you've won an initial trust. The rest of the story can build on that.

PUTTING IT ALL TOGETHER: AN OPENING THAT WORKS

The best way to see how character, conflict, specificity, and credibility can all be present in the first three paragraphs is to study a specific example. This is the opening of "Lily Red," a short story by Karen Joy Fowler:

> One day Lily decided to be someone else. Someone with a past. It was an affliction of hers, wanting this. The desire was seldom triggered by any actual incident or complaint, but seemed instead to be related to the act or prospect of lateral movement. She felt it every time a train passed. She would have traded places instantly with any person on any train. She felt it often in the car. She drove onto the freeway that ran between her job and her house and she thought about driving right past her exit and stopping in some small town wherever she happened to run out of gas and the next thing she knew, that was exactly what she had done.
>
> Except that she was stopped by the police instead. She was well beyond the city; she had been through sev-

eral cities, and the sky had darkened. The landscape flattened and she fell into a drowsy rhythm in which she and the car were both passengers in a small, impellent world defined by her headlights. It was something of a shock to have to stop. She sat in her car while the police light rotated behind her and at regular intervals she watched her hands turn red on the steering wheel. She had never been stopped by the police before. In the rearview mirror she could see the policeman talking to his radio. His door was slightly open; the light was on inside his car. He got out and came to talk to her. She turned her motor off. "Lady," he said, and she wondered if policemen on television always called women *lady* because that was what real policemen did, or if he had learned this watching television just as she had. "Lady, you were flying. I clocked you at eighty."

Eighty. Lily couldn't help but be slightly impressed. She had been twenty-five miles per hour over the limit without even realizing she was speeding. It suggested she could handle even faster speeds. "Eighty," she said contritely. "You know what I think I should do? I think I've been driving too long and I think I should just find a place to stay tonight. I think that would be best. I mean, eighty. That's too fast. Don't you think?"

Character

Lily emerges immediately as a definite personality, with individual emotions: a desire for escape, the willingness to act on her desire, a talent for introspection, a sharp and satiric observation of others, and a kind of asocial fearlessness that is not abashed at having been caught speeding, but instead is impressed with herself. Note that we aren't directly told any of this about her. Instead, we are *shown* her actions, thoughts and reactions, and from these a definite person emerges.

One way you know Lily is an individual is that it's so easy to imagine a different sort of woman having different reactions to everything that's happened so far, starting with the desire to be somebody else. A good check on the degree of individuality your character shows in your opening is the question, "Would nine out of ten people behave and think like this?" If the answer is "yes," you may not have conveyed enough of who your character actually is. She shouldn't be nine out of ten people; she should be herself.

Conflict

The very first sentence of Fowler's story sets up the expectation of change, the catalyst for conflict. Readers immediately guess that being someone else isn't going to be easy. This is a project fraught with pitfalls. It may not be possible. We suspect that other characters will object. By the first sentence of the second paragraph, someone has: the police officer clocking Lily at eighty. The reader by now has been set up to expect both conflict within Lily herself and conflict between Lily and those around her, and the rest of the story delivers on both kinds of turmoil.

Specificity

The first four sentences of this opening are unusual in that they are both expository and abstract: We're being *told* about Lily in detached language. Fowler gets away with this because she immediately strengthens the abstractions with concrete examples: "She felt it every time a train passed. She would have traded places instantly with any person on any train. She felt it often in the car. …" After that, the details are consistently specific. We see the light on inside the police car, its door open while the officer talks on the radio. We see the rotating police light turn Lily's hands red each time its beam sweeps over her. We see a very specific and quirky reaction of Lily's to being called "lady." We learn that Lily is impressed with her own speed. None of these details are the first ones that would occur to any writer; they are part of Fowler's unique perception of the situation she has created, and hence interesting.

Look at one of your own story openings. (Go ahead, dig one out of the file cabinet.) Do the first two or three paragraphs contain details of similar specificity, clear visualization, and originality? If not, are there vague or ordinary details you could rewrite to be more definite or individual?

Credible Prose

Fowler writes a sure, deft prose that relies on short sentences: More than half contain nine words or fewer. She varies these with longer sentences, five of which contain twenty-five or more words. She uses unexpected diction to pique interest, as with the "small, impellent world" defined by the moving headlights. Repetition is used for emphasis; the first three sentences are all variations of the same point, which lends it an insistence that makes us feel how much Lily wants this. The prose is light on adjectives. There are only four in the whole first paragraph, and of these, only one really registers as an adjective: "lateral." (In contrast, "actual incident," "small town," and "next thing" seem more like integral phrases.)

Does this mean that you, too, should write with short sentences, repetition for emotional emphasis, and almost no adjectives? No, of course not. But you should look at the prose in your opening paragraphs as closely as we've just looked at Fowler's, to see that it makes the same tight, controlled, interesting impression. Look for words that can come out: Cut, cut whenever you can. Look for adjectives and adverbs that can be replaced with stronger nouns and verbs. Reach for stronger or more surprising diction. Experiment with varying sentence lengths—would ending a paragraph with a very short sentence add punch? Would starting with one, as Fowler often does? Could you break up that string of six fifteen-word sentences in a row by combining two of them? How does it read now?

THE REST OF YOUR FIRST SCENE

Now you have three brilliant paragraphs (or maybe even five or eight or ten). You have a genuine character on the page. You've hinted at conflict. Your details are well chosen and concrete. You've caught your reader's attention. But a handful of paragraphs—even brilliant ones—do not constitute a scene. What will happen during the remainder of that crucial first scene?

Well, what do you want that first scene to accomplish in terms of your story? Put another way, what should be different at the end of the scene from the beginning of the scene?

Scenes in fiction are of two types: dramatic and expository. Expository scenes, which we'll discuss in more detail in the next chapter, essentially summarize action that isn't new enough or important enough to need full dramatic treatment. Suppose, for instance, you're writing a mystery novel and your detective is interviewing three neighbors of the victim, none of whom has any relevant information. Nor do any of them have anything to say important to later plot developments. Rather than write three full interviews in which nothing happens to change the basic situation, you would probably summarize those scenes in a few sentences of exposition:

> Next I talked to the neighbors. Mrs. Catalin, in 3-C, had slept through the shouting, the gunshots, the screaming. She was sleeping again when I rang her bell, and didn't appreciate being woken. Ancient and half-deaf Mr. Harrison in 3-B, on the other hand, was overjoyed to see me—or anybody—and it was twenty minutes before I could escape, having learned only that the victim "wasn't over friendly-like." 3-D, Ms. Kilgore, the fourth-grade teacher who

seemed about as home in that building as a Biblical scholar in the Combat Zone, had been in school at the time of the shooting. She'd only lived there four days, and had never met the victim. Nada.

The first scene of your short story shouldn't be a summary scene. In fact, scene one *can't* be a scene in which the situation doesn't change, because the job of scene one is to give us the initial situation. *Anything* you tell us is going to be a change from what we knew at the start of the story— nothing—and therefore the first scene should be dramatized. You can, of course, just have your characters stand around discussing a situation they're all already familiar with but we're not. However, the first scene will be much more interesting—and much easier to write—if something is different at the end of the scene than existed at the beginning. Thus, your first job in finishing that first scene is to figure out what that change might be. Here are some possibilities:

- A character discovers that a task he is starting is more complicated than he'd hoped.

- A character learns a disturbing piece of information.

- A character arrives someplace new.

- A character meets someone who will significantly alter his life; even in the first scene the new acquaintance has begun to change the character's immediate goals or ideas.

- An event occurs—a murder, a spaceship landing, the arrival of a letter—that will lead to significant change. The first scene details the event and hints at the kind of repercussions that will follow.

I could go on and on. The point is that each of these first scenes introduces a change or potential change. In addition, each is potent enough for endless variations. For instance, "A character discovers that a task he is starting is more complicated than he'd hoped" describes the first scenes *of Bonfire of the Vanities, To Kill a Mockingbird,* and "Lily Red," in which the "tasks" are campaigning in Harlem, making recluse Boo Radley come out of his house, and escaping one's ordinary life.

So—what change will be introduced in *your* first scene? In whose life? How will that person feel about it? Once you know these answers, you can build on your strong opening to finish your first scene.

A word about the way you end that first scene. The last sentence of a scene, just before the scene break, is the power position (just as the last word in a paragraph is a power position, and the last line of a chapter, and the last paragraph of a novel). Make it count. The closing sentence of a first scene should evoke some emotion—not blatantly, but through a telling detail that means more than just itself.

It's more difficult to give examples of meaningful end lines than of opening lines, because end lines only become meaningful in the context of the entire scene. But let's try anyway. The following line is the last sentence of the first scene of Alice Hoffman's novel *Seventh Heaven.* The novel is set in 1950s suburbia. The first scene deals with the problem of a vacant house on Hemlock, Street, which is going to seed and must be sold before it erodes property values. The scene also deals subtly with the changes that have come over this neighborhood since the starry-eyed young couples first moved from the city into their brand-new, all-alike tract houses. The last paragraph concerns the housewives' typical day; it ends with this sentence:

> Then they faced the mirror and took the bobby pins out of their hair and combed out their pin curls, but by the time they went back to their bedrooms their husbands were already asleep, and the fireflies were hidden between the blades of grass on their own front lawns.

This sentence is poignant because it depicts in concrete form the stagnation that has set in on Hemlock Street. Even sex, the life force, is on the verge of winking out: Wives prepare for it ritually (and after dutifully scrubbing out the bathtub), but husbands are already asleep. Nature, so dazzling to city eyes when they first moved to Hemlock Street, has likewise become invisible to those same eyes, hidden "on their own front lawns." Desire for life might, like the fireflies, still be present, but it isn't doing anybody much good.

Note that none of this is stated overtly. A hasty reader might not even pick it up. But it's there, coloring the last line of the scene with subtle emotion—loss, regret, delicate frustration.

This sentence also, incidentally, paves the way for the next scene. If there were ever a place ripe for change, it's dimmed-out and stagnant Hemlock Street. This change arrives in scene two, in the form of Nora Silk, who is unlike anyone already living in the neighborhood. And the novel is off and running.

A SPECIAL CASE: THE PROLOGUE

In some novels, the opening scene is set in its own chapter and labeled "Prologue," which is then followed by "Chapter One." This is most effective when there's a strong reason to set the prologue off by itself. Sometimes the prologue takes place a long time before the main narrative, as in Joan D. Vinge's science fiction novel *The Snow Queen*. Sometimes the prologue takes place a long time after the main narrative, as in Daphne du Maurier's *Rebecca,* in which case the entire novel becomes a flashback. Sometimes, as in Michael Crichton's bestseller *Jurassic Park,* the prologue is written from a different point of view, one which will never be used again. Occasionally a prologue consists of a real or fictional document— court summons or last will or newspaper article or personal letter—that prepares readers for the drama to come.

The advantage of a prologue, then, is twofold. It can avoid what might otherwise be a jolting transition between two scenes widely separated in time or space; the reader more or less *expects* the story to start over again after a prologue. And if it is interesting enough, a prologue can whet the appetite for the main story.

Note those two key words: *interesting enough.* To succeed, your prologue must contain a strong promise of conflict to come. Using the prologue to merely *set the scene* with passive descriptions of landscape or character background won't work. In Crichton's prologue to *Jurassic Park,* for example, a construction worker is severely mauled by an unidentified animal that, the cover picture indicates, will turn out to be a dinosaur—in contemporary Costa Rica. That certainly promises enough potential conflict to arouse readers' curiosity.

However, prologues also have disadvantages, the main one being that you must write two opening scenes, since the story actually starts twice. And even when each opening contains all the elements we've discussed, polished to a high gloss, a prologue doubles the reader's opportunity to decide she's not interested and put down your book. So if you're planning a prologue to your novel, consider carefully whether you will gain more with a prologue than you will risk. If so, spend the same time and effort on both prologue and scene one that you'd give either if it stood alone.

SUMMARY: THE VERY BEGINNING

Does all this sound like a lot of work to spend on one scene, when you still have anywhere from two to two hundred more to write? And suppose you're eager to go on to those other scenes. Should you stop your story dead to rewrite and polish your opening?

That depends. Writers compose stories in various ways. Some work best when they write like a runner racing through a haunted graveyard late at night: full speed ahead and no looking back. Others polish each scene as they write it. Still others write several variations of key scenes (such as the opening) to discover what they want to say. We'll discuss each of these techniques in later chapters. The main idea here is that at *some* point—earlier or later—it's well worth spending considerable time rewriting and polishing that first scene. You'll greatly increase the chances of an editor finishing your story.

And if you *are* one of those writers who stops to polish before going on to scene two, you'll gain a dividend. You will have made writing the rest of the story or novel much easier on yourself. This is because you now have a firmer idea of who your character is, what the conflict will be, and what the tone of the story will be. You have, by your first scene, committed to certain directions for each of these. Knowing that can keep you from wandering into different directions. How?

- When you've firmly established your character, you're less likely to weaken the story by making him do something out of character.

- When you've hinted at one source of conflict, you'll know to develop that source.

- When your rewriting and attention to specific details have established a certain tone for the story—and they inevitably will—you can stay true to that tone, forsaking all others.

This elimination of some choices can be a great help, because it allows you to focus more clearly on the remaining choices. You're like an architect who designs a house. Just as you wouldn't plan a Victorian cupola for what will be a Tudor cottage, you wouldn't have a character you've established as naive suddenly exhibit great cunning. The first scene, if not exactly a complete blueprint, is at least a preliminary sketch, with some features already chosen.

If, on the other hand, you don't want to rewrite scene one until after the first draft is complete—then don't. Build that first scene as well as you can the first time through, with the understanding that you'll tear it down later, if necessary. This—the Urban Renewal Theory of Writing

Fiction—works better for writers who discover their plot and characters only during the physical act of writing. As long as you rewrite and polish *sometime,* your first scene will become a strong foundation for the rest of your story.

Then you can build from there.

EXERCISES FOR FIRST SCENES

1. Find an anthology or magazine of short stories. Read the first sentences of each. How many hint at some future conflict or change?

2. Choose two of the stories and study their first three paragraphs. Does each opening contain an individualized character? A hint of conflict? Specific, interesting, concrete details? How do the openings differ from each other in their handling of these elements? Is there anything here you can use in your openings?

3. Do the same with the opening scenes of at least two novels you've read and admired. Study the last paragraphs of the first scenes. Do they evoke emotion through detail or dialogue? Is that emotion related to what you know the rest of the novel to be about?

4. Pull out a story you've written that you're not happy with. Study just the first three paragraphs (five if they're very short or include much dialogue). Is there an individualized person here? A hint of conflict? Specific and telling details? If not, rewrite the opening to include these things, even if you never plan to rewrite the rest of the story.

5. Pull out a story you've written that you *are* happy with. Study the prose in the first long paragraph carefully. Can you cut any words without loss of information? Are there any vague or abstract words you can replace with more definite ones? How many adjectives and adverbs are there? Are any redundant?

Can you cut some even if they're not redundant? (The ones left will have more force.) Look at the paragraph again. Did cutting improve it?

6. Look at a story you're currently writing. What changes occur from the start to the end of the first scene? If nothing does, should something? What? Does the scene's closing line evoke that change, or the necessity of change? Is it a significant line in some other way?

CHAPTER 2
THE LATER BEGINNING: YOUR SECOND SCENE

Ten years ago I wrote a terrific opening scene for a short story about a disillusioned Vietnam vet who takes to the woods and a hard-nosed dryad who resents his presence. The story had conflict, character, understated lyricism. Unfortunately, it also had only that one scene. I could never figure out what was supposed to come next. The story remains unfinished, although I haul it out and stare at it every once in a while.

This dreary occurrence is, happily, not typical. Usually when I sit down to write I know at least enough story events to fill a second scene (although I may not know *all* the events—more on that when we come to outlining). A more usual problem is whether to tell those events now or to pause to fill in background.

Suppose, for instance, you've begun a story about Jane and her husband, Sam, whose marriage is in trouble at least in part because of their fourteen-year-old daughter's problems. Your first scene is a fight between Jane and Sam over how to handle Martha's latest outrage, which is disappearing for three days and refusing to say where she's been. During the course of the fight both Jane and Sam say unforgivable things, those things lurking in the corners of every marriage that should never be hurled at each other as accusation. You're happy with the first scene—but now what?

You have three basic options for your second scene: backfill, flashback, or a continuation of story time.

BACKFILL: THE SWIMMING POOL THEORY

Backfill is basically expository background, explaining who these people are and how they got into this mess in the first place. It can be handled in two ways: as straight exposition in the author's voice or as a sort of pseudoreminiscence in the voice of the point-of-view character.

Avery Corman's popular novel *Kramer vs. Kramer,* for instance, opens in a delivery room, during the birth of the Kramers' first child. The next few scenes are backfill about the course of the pregnancy, both partners' reactions to it, the acquiring of a crib and layette and other necessities. This backfill is presented mostly as exposition and summary.

Similarly, your story might have as its second scene expository backfill about Jane and Sam's problems with Martha over the last few years.

You can also present the backfill in the voice of the point-of-view character—let's say it's Jane:

> You couldn't say this was the first time Martha had pulled this stunt, Jane thought as she picked up the magazines Sam had thrown at her. Martha had her father's temper. The least little thing and off she'd go, with no more thought for other people than a cat had. No, less—at least a cat came home to eat. At eleven years old Martha had been picked up by the police, eating from a dumpster because Jane had yelled at her about her messy bedroom. The cop had been suspicious, suspecting some sticky form of child abuse. Jane had been horrified. Martha had just gazed at them both levelly, that cold-eyed squint it seemed she'd been born with, and what could Jane do? Martha only acted like she did to hurt her mother. Jane had known then she'd be defeated by this heartbreaking, mean-eyed child. As defeated as if Martha was some throwback to her great-granddaddy's tainted blood, which in Jane's opinion she was.

Will this backfill slow down the story? Yes. Will it slow down the story too much? That's a judgement call, but here's a guideline to help you make it: the Swimming Pool Theory. This theory says that structuring fiction is like kicking off from the side of a swimming pool. The stronger and more forceful your initial kick, the longer you can glide through the water. The stronger and more forceful your opening scene, the less your reader will mind a "glide" through nondramatized backfill. In fact, the reader may even welcome the slow-down, as a contrast to a dynamite first scene. Explosives going off all the time can be wearing.

FLASHBACKS: YOU CAN GO HOME AGAIN

The Swimming Pool Theory also applies to another type of second scene, the *flashback*. For a flashback to succeed as part of your beginning, it should meet three criteria.

First, it should follow a strong opening scene, one that roots us firmly in your character's present. This means that we have enough sense of her as an individual, and of her present situation as dramatic potential, so that the flashback doesn't seem to be happening to a cipher. This passage wouldn't make a good story beginning:

> It had started to snow. Leaning wearily on the windowsill, Jane thought back to another snowy day, the day Martha had been born. Jane had been only eighteen, scared stiff that she would die or maybe that she wouldn't, when the pains started ...

We know nothing yet about Jane's present, and hence have no reason to be interested in her past, so this flashback won't work as a first scene. It might, however, work well as a second scene, if it follows the fight between Jane and Sam about the kind of girl Martha is growing up to be.

In addition, the second-scene flashback should bear some clear relation to the first scene we've just witnessed. Following a fight over Martha's behavior, we easily accept as relevant the scene of Martha's birth. If, however, the flashback had concerned Jane's school days, the story might seem to jump around too much for a beginning, when readers are still easing in. Don't make them jump in both time and subject matter right away. Give them a flashback that deepens their knowledge of the previous scene, rather than distracting them from it.

Finally, don't let your readers get lost in time. Indicate clearly how much earlier the flashback scene took place. There's nothing a reader hates worse than assuming flashback events occurred earlier the same day and then discovering—sometimes chapters later—that, no, they actually occurred years ago. Everything the reader thought he knew about the situation is in fact wrong. Use clear transitions such as "Two weeks ago" or "Doug's childhood in San Diego had been different." Or make sure the numbers add up, as in the above example. If we've learned in scene one that Martha is fourteen, and if Jane is now recalling her birth, then the flashback must be fourteen years ago.

A writer always pays a price for flashbacks. *Any* flashback, no matter how well written or interesting, will distance your reader from the action. This is because flashbacks shatter the illusion that the reader is a fly on the wall, witnessing events as they happen, *right now*. The flashback is not happening right now—it is, by definition, already over. Are you more thrilled by a kiss you experience today or one you remember from a year ago? Flashbacks are not as immediate as story time. Even so, the flashback can be a good choice for a second scene *if you gain more in depth and clarity than you lose in immediacy.*

CONTINUING IN STORY TIME: CONTROLLING CONFLICT

Your third choice for a second scene is simply to go on with the story, dramatizing whatever happens next to whoever is your point-of-view character. Maybe Sam slams out of the house and Jane goes upstairs to confront Martha. Or maybe Martha, having overheard her parents fighting, runs off again, this time three hundred miles away to Memphis. Or maybe Sam packs his things and moves out, and on the way to a hotel his Volvo is hit by a bus.

Any of these scenes could work. Or they could not work, depending on how well you manage the issue of conflict.

Your second scene in story time will undoubtedly have some conflict in it. Certainly all three choices above do. What you want to avoid, however, is the sense that every single scene in your story or novel is going to consist of a shouting match or a personal crisis. When every scene is laden with intense conflict, the story becomes monotonous (even explosions can come to seem routine). Worse, it becomes unrealistic. The reader knows that life may consist of one damn thing after another, but not all the damn things are of the same intensity. Sometimes people stop to catch their breath, brood on what just happened, plan what to do next, carry on previous plans from some previous crisis. Sometimes things just plain slow down. If, in your story, they never slow down, the story will seem unrealistic.

On the other hand, you don't want the conflict to slow down so much that the reader thinks, "Is that all? Isn't anything else going to happen?" Hamlet may have postponed meaningful action for five acts while he was "sicklied o'er with the pale cast of thought," but while he was so occupied, other characters were acting out their own conflicts. Things kept happening in Denmark. They should in your story or novel, too.

What does this have to do with writing a second scene in story time? It means that one consideration for that second scene should be the level of conflict it contains. Let's look at our three choices again.

JANE, MARTHA, SAM: THREE SECOND SCENES

If Jane confronts Martha and the resulting fight is about the same length and bitterness of the one Jane just had with Sam, you will have in effect written the first scene all over again. Two fights, on the same topic, of the same intensity, one after the other. This might very well seem redundant to the reader, who may wonder if this whole story is going to consist of domestic arguments. The conflict level is too close to the first scene.

What could you do about this, if you wanted to keep Jane's point of view and also keep that intense opening fight with Sam? You could make the confrontation with Martha of a lesser intensity. This time Jane keeps her temper, and the argument is short, controlled, and quiet—a contrast to the first scene. Or you could find something else for Jane to do in story time. Maybe she gets on the phone and tries to find a therapist for Martha. Maybe she calls up her own mother to complain. Maybe she tries to distract herself from domestic disharmony by gardening or getting drunk or going to church (note that each of these choices paints a very different Jane). A quieter second scene avoids melodrama. It cools down the conflict so that the characters—and your readers—have time to react to it. What they decide to do about their reactions form the next stage of the plot.

Or maybe you want Martha's point of view. She's overheard her parents fighting about her, she can't stand it anymore, and she decides to run away. This is obviously a reaction to the conflict in scene one. In scene two, you show Martha stealthily packing her things, taking two hundred dollars from a hiding place her parents don't know she knows about, and sneaking out of the house with her suitcase. You show her hailing a taxi, buying a bus ticket, and striking up a conversation with a woman in the bus station, who will later turn out to be an off-duty police officer.

This scene has tension (Will Martha make it out of town without being stopped? Will she be safe if she does?), but it also lowers the intensity from the previous fight scene. Again, conflict has been cooled down for contrast—without sacrificing story movement (the off-duty officer will report Martha as a runaway).

The third choice, Sam's moving out and getting hit by a bus, doesn't cool down the conflict. Instead, it introduces a subplot. First we had domestic difficulties and a wayward child. Now we've added medical problems. Sam gets a compound femoral fracture and will spend four weeks in traction, during which time he'll meet a fellow patient, a miner, dying of black lung disease. Sam will eventually be changed by this encounter, in surprising ways.

Will the introduction of this subplot introduce competing conflict that will distract the reader? Will the story start to seem too melodramatic? That depends on how you write it. If the accident with the bus is replete with shouting and pain and gore, it may rival in intensity the first scene.

But if you keep the accident itself brief and factual and concentrate instead on Sam's attempts at bravery despite pain, and on the conversations he has with various medical people trying to help him, you could attain a very nice contrast to scene one. The fight with Jane was destructive behavior: relationships unraveling, conflict mounting. Once hit by a bus (and away from his wife), Sam shows admirable behavior; human interactions are compassionate; people work together against conflict from an outside act. The subplot has its own conflict, but it varies in both intensity and type from the first scene's conflict. It also grows out of that first scene (if Sam hadn't been moving out, he wouldn't have tangled with the bus).

CHOOSING THE ACTION
FOR YOUR SECOND SCENE

The point here is that your second scene in story time must both carry the action forward and control the conflict level. The best way to choose a scene to do that is to keep a single question firmly in mind: *What do these people want?*

In fiction, something must be at stake. People can't just move through their ordinary lives, because fiction isn't ordinary life—not even when it's trying to look as if it is. Fiction is life rearranged into clearer patterns and meanings than real life usually yields. In fiction, people try to accomplish things, or cope with things, or just make things go away. They want something, even if it's just to be left alone.

Grasping this truth can greatly simplify plotting your story or novel, which just means deciding what will happen in the scenes of your story. Ask yourself, "What does each of my characters want?" Once you know—I usually make a short list—you can figure out how these particular individuals would go about getting it. This in turn suggests scenes.

Jane, for instance, wants her daughter to be a model child. She has a firm idea in her head about how a fourteen-year-old girl should behave, and what she wants is for Martha to stick to it. Jane sets about trying to get this by fighting with Martha, fighting with Sam, easing her own frustration through complaining to her friends, and drinking too much. These are not necessarily the best methods to get what Jane wants, but they're the methods she knows and she's using them.

What does Sam want? He wants to avoid any trouble; it makes him feel too awful. So he refuses to confront Martha (this is what Jane's so furious about), he works late at the office, he turns on the TV the moment he gets home to avoid talking, and finally he moves out. He didn't foresee the bus.

What does Martha want? She wants her parents to stop hassling her. She wants to feel okay inside, which she hardly ever does. Hanging out with older kids and doing drugs for three days makes her feel okay for a short while—if the older kids are okay and they accept her, that must mean she's okay, too. But eventually she has to come home. Her mother is terrible about the missing three days, which makes Martha feel awful. So she splits. *That* will end the hassling.

It's easy, once you know what these people want, to see all kinds of potential scenes for this story. Choose a second one from the possibilities, depending on whose story you're concentrating on (in a novel, maybe all three people's stories). Then adjust the conflict level to contrast with the first.

WHO *ARE* THESE PEOPLE? INTRODUCING AND DEVELOPING YOUR CHARACTERS

So far we've talked about writing the first two scenes to develop conflict and imply change. Notice, however, that in everything I've said so far is an implicit assumption: *Different characters will have different kinds of conflicts and changes.* The Jane who reacts to the fight with her husband by going to church to pray is not the same Jane who reacts by pouring three fingers of Scotch. Another Jane, in fact, never would have had the fight in the first place. She would have simply pretended not to notice that Martha was gone for three days.

This means that as your beginning scenes portray conflict, they also portray character. The two cannot be separated. A character creates or reacts to conflict in ways dictated by the kind of person he is. How you show him acting will in turn create further conflict—or alleviate it. "Character is plot," Henry James said, and this is what he meant. Every paragraph in your story should accomplish two goals: advance the story (the plot), and develop your characters as real, individual, complex, and memorable human beings.

Most of this character development will probably go on in the middle of your story or novel (and we'll address it there in greater depth). But even in the beginning scenes, before we understand all the reasons behind your characters' behavior, they shouldn't be ciphers. They should show us early on that they're people interesting enough to justify investing our reading time in their problems.

The first step in creating characters who are not ciphers is for them not to be ciphers to *you*. Sometimes a new writer will work out an interesting plot for her detective story or thriller or romance or fantasy novel, and then immediately start writing. Instead, spend some time thinking about your characters. What makes them individual? Where did they grow up? What was their childhood like? What is their life like now? Notice that these questions don't focus on what the characters want in terms of the story. These questions go back further than that, before the story events began to happen. These are questions about who your people are when they're *not* in the story.

"Does that matter?" you might ask. If this information isn't going to be in the story, why bother to think about it? Mark Twain had the answer to that. One of his nineteen rules for writing fiction required "that the personages in a tale shall always be alive, except in the case of corpses, and that always the reader shall be able to tell the corpses from the others." Imagining backgrounds for your characters helps bring them alive in your mind. The next step is to bring them alive on the page—right away, in the first scenes.

At this point, characters reveal who they are in six ways, some of which we've already discussed.

Actions They Initiate

Fighting viciously with one's spouse, packing to move out, running away on a bus—all are major actions that not only advance the plot but also start to characterize Jane, Sam, and Martha. However, actions alone can't fully develop character. That's because the same action can spring from different motives. Is Jane fighting with the passive Sam because she's genuinely frightened about her daughter, or is Martha's behavior just one more excuse for Jane's real motive, which is to bully Sam? In the opening scenes, we probably won't find out. Such complex motivations are usually made clear in the middle of a story or novel. Still, actions are a good way to start showing us who these people are.

Reactions to Other Characters' Actions

When one character says or does something, another character's reactions to this event can effectively characterize both of them. A chain reaction starts. Consider Jane and Sam, for instance:

> Jane took a swig of Dr Pepper. "I wish you weren't so spineless around that girl, Sam. She just snarls you around her little finger is what she does. Every single time."
>
> Sam took his nine-iron out of his bag and squinted along its length. It needed cleaning. He reached for the cloth.
>
> "She's failing algebra and English and I don't know what else. Seems like she just can't get her mind on school long enough to even show up regular. Sam, are you *listening* to me?"
>
> Her tone was unmistakable. So was the angle of her cigarette, the tap of her knee against the table, the ridgy look to her neck muscles. Sam trusted neck muscles. "I'm going out to buy golf balls," he said quickly, and went.

Sam's reactions to Jane's actions tell us a lot about him.

Dialogue

Again, at a story's beginning, a character's dialogue probably is not going to reveal much about his deeper motives, fears, ambiguities, strengths, and other fundamental qualities. But it can— and should—reveal basics of class, education, and surface personality. You can accomplish this even when a character does something routine. The following characters, for instance, are all ordering in a diner:

> "I shall have a cup of tea, black, and a small salad. No tomatoes, as tomatoes upset my digestion."

"Gimme pie and coffee, sweetie. Got any apple?"

"The diet plate, the one with cottage cheese and a pear half and tea with lemon and ... and ... oh, hell, and a banana split."

"I don't suppose you have any pie that's really home-baked, do you?"

"Is the chicken free-range? Is the zucchini grown organically? Don't you *know?*"

Do you have different impressions of each of these characters?

Thoughts

The thoughts of the point-of-view character can reveal an enormous amount about her—including things she may not know herself. Look again at that backfill in Jane's point of view:

> You couldn't say this was the first time Martha had pulled this stunt, Jane thought as she picked up the magazines Sam had thrown at her. Martha had her father's temper. The least little thing and off she'd go, with no more thought for other people than a cat had. No, less—at least a cat came home to eat. At eleven years old Martha had been picked up by the police, eating from a dumpster because Jane had yelled at her about her messy bedroom. The cop had been suspicious, suspecting some sticky form of child abuse. Jane had been horrified. Martha had just gazed at them both levelly, that cold-eyed squint it seemed she'd been born with, and what could Jane do? Martha only acted like she did to hurt her mother. Jane had known then she'd be defeated by this heartbreaking, mean-eyed child. As defeated as if Martha was some throwback to her great-granddaddy's tainted blood, which in Jane's opinion she was.

Jane's thoughts here, in addition to supplying background information on this family, reveal her character. Jane thinks she's a victim ("Martha only acted like she did to hurt her mother") of a biological accident ("her great-granddaddy's tainted blood"), completely innocent. We readers, however, see a woman who takes no responsibility for her daughter's behavior, shows no compassion for Martha's adolescent problems, and perceives herself at the center of everybody else's universe.

Gestures and Body Language

Lighting a cigarette to show nervousness may have become cliché, but there is still a wealth of body language you can use to individualize your character. The woman who kisses everybody on both cheeks (she's not French), the child who habitually walks into walls in a personal fog (she's not blind), the man who clutches the steering wheel so hard he's bent it (he's not Arnold Schwarzenegger)—they reveal something about the inner person by their outer mannerisms. Similarly, the man who delivers a speech while gazing over his buddy's left shoulder might ordinarily be an easygoing guy, but at this particular moment he clearly feels uncomfortable.

Appearance

This one is easily misused, falling into stereotype: the beautiful blonde heroine, the jolly fat man, the crazed killer with wild eyes and a scar down one cheek. It's more effective to characterize through aspects of physical appearance that your character can control. How she dresses, whether her haircut is fashionable, which newspaper she carries, the state of her shoes—all can be used to reveal aspects of her personality. Think of Laurie Colwin's laid-back heroine in "My Mistress," a successful economist wearing "a pair of very old, broken shoes with tassels, the backs of which are held together with electrical tape." Obviously this is not a woman who values the opinion of the world.

Similarly, your character has at least some degree of control over her living space, and so her surroundings can also be used to reveal her personality. (The Colwin character's study is "bare of ornament and actually cheerless.")

PUTTING IT ALL TOGETHER: CHARACTERS WE WANT TO READ MORE ABOUT

If you rely on just one or two of these methods to characterize your people, you're missing chances to make your beginning snag readers into wanting to know more. Here, for example, is a brief passage from a writer who is not doing his job. By relying only on dialogue to characterize, he has conveyed only the minimal sense of what these people are really like:

> "Who's there?" Louise called.
>
> "It's me. Allen."
>
> "Come on in, Allen."
>
> He entered the room. "I came to see how you're doing. Since the divorce."
>
> "That's nice of you. I'm fine."
>
> "I wish I were," he said.
>
> "I'm sorry? I didn't hear you."
>
> "I said I wish I were fine."
>
> "Things aren't going too well for you?" she asked.
>
> "I miss you, Louise."
>
> "I'm sorry about that, but I think you better leave."

Watch what happens when the dialogue is left intact but is supplemented with character's thoughts, appearance, gestures, actions, and reactions:

> "Who's there?" Louise called. Damn, she had forgotten to latch the back door again.
>
> "It's me, Allen," a voice called uncertainly.
>
> "Come on in, Allen." She folded her arms across her chest and watched him pick his way across the basement, through the mounds of unwashed laundry, piles of kids' toys, a dog puddle she hadn't gotten around to cleaning up yet. He wore

a T-shirt too big for his spindly body and the most ridiculous hat she'd ever seen.

"I came to see how you're doing," Allen said. His eyes darted nervously around the room. "Since the divorce."

Louise smiled nastily. "That's nice of you. I'm fine." She waved her hand at the room. As if on cue, a pile of laundry toppled over.

Allen said nothing for a long moment. Then he said, quick and low, "I wish I were."

Louise cupped her hand elaborately over one ear and leaned forward. "I'm sorry? I didn't hear you."

He swallowed hard. "I said I wish I were fine."

She grinned. "Things aren't going too well for you?"

The dog came down the basement stairs and lifted a leg against the dryer. Allen looked as if he were trying not to notice. "I miss you, Louise."

"I'm sorry about that," Louise said, her voice rich with satisfaction. "But I think you better leave."

Now we know these people *much* better. To really see how much characterization can be achieved by the details surrounding dialogue, consider yet a third version. Again, the dialogue has not been changed by so much as a single word.

"Who's there?" Louise called. She could feel her heart slam against her chest wall. The figure moved closer, out of the darkness of the kitchen.

"It's me. Allen."

There was a long pause. Louise picked up her embroidery and clutched it against her breasts. She fought to keep her voice steady. "Come on in, Allen."

He was already in. She saw that he wore his usual Saturday night outfit: jeans, boots, leather jacket. He crossed the rug to stand so close to her rocker that she could smell the whiskey, a faint blurry odor around his thighs. She bit her lip.

"I came to see how you're doing," he said softly. "Since the divorce."

"That's nice of you," Louise quavered, because she couldn't think what else to say, couldn't think at all. His belt buckle glittered beside her cheek. "I'm fine."

He touched a curl at her nape. She flinched, and he smiled. "I wish I were."

"I'm sorry?" Louise whispered. "I didn't hear you." The room was unaccountably full of buzzing.

He squatted beside her chair, his face inches from hers. He was still smiling. "I said I wish I were fine."

"Things aren't... going too well for you?" The buzzing grew louder. His teeth looked very white, pointed, and sharp.

One finger caressed the top of her shoulder. "I miss you, Louise."

"I'm sorry about that," she gasped. "But I think you better leave."

Obviously, this Louise and this Allen are entirely different characters from the previous pair. The difference comes from details of gesture, appearance, tone, thoughts and reaction that color the dialogue. The more of this you can get into your beginning scenes, the better initial sense we'll have of your characters—and the more likely we'll be to want to read more of their story.

A CAST OF THOUSANDS: INTRODUCING MORE CHARACTERS

So far, we've mostly considered scenes with only two or three characters. But suppose your book is going to be immense, with a dozen major characters, each with individual quirks and important roles to play in the plot. Or suppose there are only three major characters in your story, but ten secondary ones whom you don't want the reader to confuse with each other. How quickly should your beginning introduce additional characters, and in what detail?

As a rule of thumb, don't throw too many characters at your reader in the first scene. He'll become confused and irritated. Hold the first scene to three named people, if you can. If it's a crowd scene—a parade, a political rally, a wedding—either let everyone else mill around nameless, or accept that the reader won't remember who the others are and you'll have to reintroduce them later.

In subsequent scenes, introduce characters only as they come onstage to do something meaningful. Rather than stop the action dead to explain who these people are, give us the bare minimum ("He saw his cousin Joe across the room") and let the character establish himself through some characteristic or significant action. *Then* we'll be interested enough to absorb his background. ("He couldn't believe what Joe had just done. But, then, Joe had been doing outrageous things all his life. Growing up together in Clayton County, as close as brothers, Joe and he had always …")

What you want to avoid is introducing each character with an expository capsule biography, as if they were Miss America contestants. ("Lovely Miss Arkansas is a junior at State studying veterinary medicine and music, and hopes for a career working with children in her beautiful hometown of Little Rock.") If it's vital that we know something about a character the minute he enters, give us that information as briefly as possible. ("Dr. Rawlins had been the town's only doctor for twenty years.") But keep it short, and save the rest until it becomes relevant (the facts that Dr. Rawlins graduated from Yale Medical in 1915, had been a brilliant wartime surgeon but had been gassed at Chateau-Thierry and never fully recovered, and is inexplicably married to the daughter of the town drunk, a shrewish woman who belittles him constantly). Better yet, bring the wife onstage and let us see her shrewishness, if it's relevant.

One effective way to prepare for the entrance of a character who's not in the first scene is to have other characters talk or think about her before she arrives. By chapter eighteen *of Anna Karenina,* when Anna finally shows up, we're very interested in this woman whom no one can praise enough. Will she really be able to straighten out her brother's troubled family? Will she really be so intelligent and tactful and charming? Our curiosity has been skillfully whetted.

The same tactic can work to prepare for less pivotal characters. If the heroine of a romance novel hears three or four times that her new boss will be very demanding and difficult to work for, when he strides into the office for the first time we already anticipate interesting interactions between them.

How many people, total, can you cram into a story? There's no real answer to that. Long novels, obviously, can include hundreds of characters (consider *Gone With the Wind* or *War and Peace).* Short stories should probably concentrate on three or four, at most, to be developed with some individuality. There also may be various unnamed "spear carriers," (such as the waitress who takes the protagonist's breakfast order), who don't need to be turned into individuals at all. They're animate furniture in the story, which is fine. Drawing too much attention to their individual quirks and histories might actually work against the story by distracting focus from your major characters. The art of fiction, like the art of stage magicians, is one of directing the audience's attention to what you want them to see.

But if there's no maximum number of characters for a story, there *is* a minimum. It's almost impossible to write a story with only one character. Without someone to talk to and interact with, the solitary character is reduced to reminiscences, philosophical musings, and speculations. Since none of these happens in story time, the effect is to distance the reader from the story itself. Even Jack London, in his classic "To Build a Fire," included a second character in the form of the dog so that the protagonist, who's trying not to freeze to death in the winter wilderness, could have someone to talk to about his situation.

A short story with two characters is certainly possible, but it, too, isn't easy. Often the two characters get into some snarl or problem, each becomes locked into his position, and you have an impasse. Introducing a third character can provide the catalyst to get things moving again. The third character does something that forces one, or both, of the originals to react, altering his position.

For example, in Flannery O'Connor's story "Everything That Rises Must Converge," Julian and his mother are locked in long-standing battle over practically everything: her racism, his ingratitude, her provincialism, his rudeness, her hat, his joblessness. For the first two-thirds of the story these positions—pathetic, hilarious, and appalling—are explored. But the possibility of change only enters the story with the arrival of a third character, the black woman on the bus, whose interactions with Julian's mother lead to events that force both Julian and his mother to actually look at themselves.

If you've started a two-person story and it seems to be going nowhere, think about introducing a catalytic third character.

THE BEGINNING AND ALL THE REST

This chapter and the preceding one have focused on only the first two scenes of your story or novel, which is in a way artificial: Those two scenes don't exist in a vacuum. Part of their function is to prepare the reader for the rest of the story.

They do this by making the implicit promise to your reader. By the time your reader has finished your first two scenes, she knows (1) what kind of story this is—domestic drama, political thriller, police procedural, etc.; (2) what general type of conflict you're promising—anything from suburban marriage problems to worldwide threat of alien invasion; (3) what tone the story takes toward its characters—ironic, detached, affectionate, heroic, melodramatic, gritty; and (4) whether the main character is someone the reader should like, identify with, or just observe. From all of this, your reader has absorbed your basic promise: *Read this and you'll be amused.* Or *Read this and you'll be scared.* Or *Read this and you'll see this human conflict in a new light.* Or *Read this and you'll experience exciting lives you wish you led.* Your reader might not be able to articulate all this. She might not *know* she's absorbed your promise. But she has—and she'll hold you to it throughout the story.

The major function of a beginning, then, is to set up the implicit promise that you will develop in the middle and fulfill at the end. But the most important point I want to make in this chapter—the point I really want you to absorb, even if you disagree with me about everything else—is that your first scenes must not function *only* as setup. If you think of them as something you and the reader must "get through" so that there's enough background to understand the story, which, like world peace, still lies ahead—if you think that, your story will fail. No matter *how* good the rest of it is.

Your beginning must function as an interesting reading experience in itself, full of character and situation and pleasing language. It must claim its reader's attention in its own right, even as you make the implicit promise that you'll fulfill later. You must think of your beginning— forgive the paradox—as an end in itself, not merely a means to an end.

That's what will keep the rest of us reading and eager to see what comes next.

MORE EXERCISES FOR BEGINNINGS

1. Find an anthology of short stories. Read the first page of each. Which ones made you want to read more? Go back and study those beginnings. What specifically caught your attention?

2. Pull out stories you've written or are in the process of writing. Are the same elements you identified in question one present in your stories? If not, do you see any way to revise the openings to include them?

3. Turn to a story or novel you've already read and know fairly well. Pick one in the same broad genre as what you write (literary mainstream, thriller, glitter romance, mystery, science fiction, etc.). Read the first two scenes. Is the second scene backfill, a flashback, or a continuation of story time? Does the second scene continue the conflict, cool down the conflict, or introduce a subplot with new conflict? How are transitions handled? Is there anything here you can use?

4. Look again at those same two scenes. How many characters are there? How do we learn about each—through dialogue, thoughts, actions, appearance, reactions, gestures, expository biography? How are new characters introduced?

5. Look now at one of your own stories. Do you use as many methods for characterizing your people? Make a list of every characteristic you've implied about your protagonist in scene one. Don't include things you know about her but haven't indicated yet; confine the list to what's there. Study the list. Does it add up to an interesting first impression or to a bland and generic one? What's individual about this person? How could you indicate it on the page?

CHAPTER 3
HELP FOR BEGINNINGS: EARLY REVISION

"**W**ell begun is half done."

I don't know that I actually believe this aphorism. A good beginning to a story or novel isn't nearly half the work, especially if you're one of those writers to whom beginnings come easily, and getting stuck thereafter comes with equal ease. But even if a good beginning doesn't equal "half done," it's nothing to be sneered at, either. You now have two strong scenes. You've established the tone of your story. You know a lot about your characters—ideally, more than you've already shown. You've started conflict of some type burning, and there's plenty of fuel left.

Pat yourself on the back. You're on your way.

But what if you're *not*? What if you've written one scene, or two or three, but you really don't like them?

It's easy to say "Rewrite"; it's not always so easy to do. You read over your first scenes, vaguely dissatisfied but unable to say why. You stare at the first page, chewing on the end of your pen or tapping the side of your keyboard. An easy thought settles into your mind: There's a better opening for this story. Somewhere. You should revise. But you can't think of how to write the scene differently. If you *could* have thought of a better opening, you'd have written it that way in the first place. Besides, you shrink from the thought of revision. How do you know you'll end up with something better this time?

You don't, of course. But there are plenty of ways to make revision feel less like anxiety-producing indecisiveness and more like an interesting experiment—and out of this experiment can come a much stronger opening.

Set aside an hour or two. During that time, write several short openings to the same story, writing very rapidly, keeping each to between three and five paragraphs. Don't try to consciously judge these openings. Instead, keep producing variations by deliberately altering either narrative mode or point of entrance into the story (more on this to come). Once you've done this a few times, you'll become quite adept at producing these by simply moving methodically through the possibilities. And, inevitably, one of the variations will click in your mind, and you'll feel that sense of rightness and eagerness—"Yes, this is it!"— that is one of the major pleasures of writing fiction.

VARYING NARRATIVE MODE: CINDERELLA REDUX

All fiction is created out of five different ways of presenting information to the reader, called *narrative modes:* dialogue, description, action, thoughts, and exposition. Some writers rely more extensively on one mode than on others. Hemingway makes heavy use of dialogue, while romance writers often include lots of description of characters' appearance, clothes, and homes. A complete story will use all five modes, but very often the opening scene is characterized by the predominance of one mode (you have to start *somewhere*).

For example, Tom Wolfe's bestselling novel *Bonfire of the Vanities* opens with dialogue:

"And then say what? Say, 'Forget you're hungry, forget you got shot ina back by some racist cop—Chuck was here? Chuck come up to Harlem—' "

"No, I'll *tell* you what—"

" 'Chuck come up to Harlem and—' "

"I'll *tell* you what—"

"Say, 'Chuck come up to Harlem and gonna take care a business for the black community'?"

That does it.

This dialogue, it's important to note, is about race and class relations in New York City. It's also pretty confusing. Both these points are important because the dialogue thus sets the stage for the novel as a whole, which portrays big-time confusion among social classes in a city that no longer functions the way it's supposed to.

Other stories start with description of a setting, person, or object that will have thematic significance. Or with a character performing some action that both launches the plot and offers insight into her as a person. Or with thoughts presented in the point-of-view character's voice. Or with exposition (this is the trickiest), in which facts are told to the reader in summary form rather than dramatized.

Once you understand the five narrative modes, you can easily write five miniopenings, letting the focus of the narrative mode spark ideas and thoughts that might not have occurred to you otherwise. As always, it's easiest to examine this process through example. We need to use a story everyone already knows, so let's choose "Cinderella." You are retelling "Cinderella," and you can't come up with an interesting opening. The traditional beginning uses exposition, summarizing events in a brief lecture:

Once upon a time there was a man with a beautiful daughter and a beloved wife. His wife died, and after a year of grief the man married again. His new wife was beautiful but selfish and vain. She and her two daughters, who were just like her, made life very hard for the motherless girl. They made her do all the washing and cleaning and cooking. After the man unexpectedly died, things became even worse for the poor child. Her stepmother made her move out of her pretty bedroom and sleep in the cinders on the hearth. From this she became known as "Cinderella."

You don't want to start your version this way. It's already been done, and besides, you don't find it very exciting. You rewrite the opening, focusing on dialogue:

"Cinderella! Have you finished the laundry yet?"

"N-no, ma'am, I was scrubbing the hearth...."

Her stepmother glared at her. "That should have been done hours ago! You're a lazy, undisciplined girl!"

"Please, ma'am, the hearth was so filthy after Cook roasted that whole boar—"

"Silence! I will not be contradicted in my own house!"

Once it was my house, Cinderella thought—but she didn't dare say that out loud.

Better? More interesting? That depends partly, of course, on your taste. Let's say you're still not pleased with it. You try a different version—and a different protagonist, who just popped into your head as you started your rapid writing—this time relying on action:

Cindy held the iron flat on the front panel of her stepsister's T-shirt. Two seconds, four, six, eight. The cloth began to smoke around the edges of the iron. Ten, twelve, fourteen. Cindy lifted the iron. A triangular scorch mark seared the exact center of Axel Rose's face. She picked up the T-shirt and held it critically to the light. The scorch went clear through the fabric. Cindy smiled. Forbid *her* to go to the rock concert, would they?

Better? That's still not the story you want to write? Try starting with description:

> The three clones *had* to look alike: They shared identical genetic blueprints. But the minds that Central had transferred into the cloned bodies had belonged to three different women. There stood Anastasia in black jeans, silver-plated vest open to her navel, and mirrorshades. Next to her Drusilla looked almost bulky in her plain bolo-cloth work clothes and boots, the boots caked with what Danforth suspected was cow manure. And Cindy! Were ruffles back in style on Earth? Cindy wore real pink silk—gods, the cost—at neck, sleeves, waist, hem. Her necklace and earrings were bloodstones, vivid red, the same shade as her ear paint. Danforth thought she looked like a massacre in a lingerie shop.

Maybe science fiction isn't your thing (although at least four different science-fiction writers have updated "Cinderella" for the space age). Try an opening based on a character's thoughts, this one aimed at preteens:

> It wasn't fair. No, it *wasn't*. She tried just as hard as her sisters, she did her schoolwork and her share of the dishes without being nagged (well, not too much) and mowed the lawn every third time. Since last year she even did her own laundry, which was more than Annie and Dru did. But did her parents care? Nooooooo. Just because she was thirteen and the twins were an ancient fourteen (big deal), they got to go to the dance and she didn't. Well, if they thought she was dumb enough to believe that was the real reason, they had another thing coming. Cindy knew better. It was because Annie and Dru were Mary's real daughters and she was just a stepdaughter. Dad spent all this time telling her they were just one big happy family, all the kids treated the

same—yeah, sure. Then *this* happens. Annie and Dru go dancing, and poor little Cindy gets to stay home and watch reruns of *Cosby*. Real fair.

Now you have five openings for the same story. And while these openings for "Cinderella" are tongue-in-cheek, five narrative-mode variations for *your* story will probably produce one beginning that feels right.

If not, try varying your point of entry.

LITERARY RELOCATION: STARTING OVER IN A DIFFERENT PLACE

Remember Jane, Sam, and Martha? In the last chapter, we considered opening their story with the fight between the parents over Martha's behavior. But maybe that opening isn't working. Again working quickly and briefly, try writing a beginning that opens either earlier or later than the fight itself. Some possibilities, depending on who you've decided to make the point-of-view character:

- a scene in which Martha wakes up sick, dirty, and starving in a filthy room she doesn't recognize (earlier than the fight)

- a scene in which Martha is brought home by the police after her three days' absence (earlier)

- a scene in which Jane confronts Martha, who has overheard her parents' fighting (later)

- a scene in which Sam is hit by the bus (later)

- a scene in which Martha sneaks out of the house (later)

Do any of those strike sparks in your mind? Usually a story will be improved by starting later in the action rather than earlier, but maybe for *your* story that won't be true. Whichever scene you decide to open with, your material will be richer for the ideas sparked by experimenting with alternatives.

A FINAL WORD ON REVISION: THE TEMPTATION TO POLISH FOREVER

In Gail Godwin's novel *Violet Clay,* Violet's Uncle Ambrose is a novelist who has been working on his second book for decades. He has seventy-five pages written, which he keeps revising over and over, occasionally reading them to appreciative women. He never gets the rest of the book written.

Once you have one or two good scenes, it can seem so much easier to polish them—sharpening details, switching sentence order, adding grace notes—than to write the next scene. Here are concrete words, and what comes next is just amorphous hints swirling in your head. Much more pleasant to improve the known than to launch out upon the unknown.

This temptation must be resisted. Even if you are one of those writers I mentioned before, who revises as you go along, making each scene as good as you can before you add the next, you must develop a sense of what's *good enough* to build on. Polish your first scene—but don't spend longer than, say, two weeks on it. After the book is finished, you'll have another crack at revision. For now, grit your teeth and move on.

If you're the other kind of writer who prefers to race through first drafts without interruption, this is easier. You won't be tempted to over-revise (tempted to do *what?),* even though in scene one your heroine is childless and in scene two, the next day, she has six-year-old twins. You'll encounter other kinds of reluctances later on.

Whichever kind you are, you now have a solid beginning—to your manuscript and to your writing process. Now it's time to move on to the middle.

STILL MORE EXERCISES FOR BEGINNINGS

Pull out a story of yours that has at least the first few scenes completed. Write five different opening scenes for the story, each no more than three to six paragraphs, focusing on:

1. The description of some object of importance to the scene.

2. Your point-of-view character engaged in some significant, unexpected action.

3. An outrageous opinion held by the point-of-view character, expressed inside her head in her own words—something she would never tell a living soul (everybody has these).

4. Six lines of dialogue between two characters (three lines each) who are arguing about something that will be important to the plot.

5. A description of the room where the first scene occurs. Focus on details that will have thematic significance and/or that tell us something about the owner's personality.

Did you like any of these openings better than your original? Did writing them spark any ideas for the story? If not, go back to your original opening.

PART TWO

Middles

····················

CHAPTER 4
THE MIDDLE: STAYING ON TRACK

"In the middle of the journey of life," wrote Dante Alighieri in *The Inferno*, "I came to myself within a dark wood where the straight way was lost. Ah, how hard it is to tell of that wood, savage and harsh and dense, the thought of which renews my fear. So bitter is it that death is hardly more."

Dante was having trouble with middles (a problem he eventually did resolve, with a little Outside help). He isn't alone. Many writers find themselves eager to begin their stories. They plunge right into their plot or setting or characters. Enthusiasm is high. The writer is still in love with whatever idea prompted him to begin a novel in the first place, and this is the honeymoon.

Then he hits the middle of the story. Like Dante, he becomes overwhelmed. Things look dense, savage, and harsh. Paths disappear. Guidelines don't seem to offer enough guidance. Discouraged, the writer comes to agree with W. Somerset Maugham, who wrote, "There are three rules for writing a novel. Unfortunately, no one knows what they are."

What makes middles so hard? Sometimes you have so much vital information that you can't figure out how to include it all (especially in a short story). Sometimes you can't think of enough interesting events to get you plausibly to the ending you've already envisioned (especially in a novel). Choices rush over you. In what order should the scenes occur?

How many points of view can you use? How will you show that your character undergoes a genuine change? What about those two events that happen simultaneously in two different cities—which should you show first? The story seems to be self-destructing in your mind. You can't imagine why anybody would want to read it. *You* don't. The honeymoon is over.

Does this all sound too gloomy? If so, perhaps you're one of those fortunate writers who doesn't have trouble with middles. You can breathe a sigh of relief and keep on typing. But if you have felt that savage wood, it's a help to know that there are lights in the forest that can help.

DEVELOPING THE PROMISE

The middle of the story can be defined (perhaps arbitrarily) as everything after the introduction of the main characters/conflict and before the climax. Note how slippery this definition is. In a very short story, the main conflict may be underway by the second paragraph, which may be part of the first scene—especially if the story has only two or three scenes. The beginning seamlessly becomes the middle, with no real dividing point.

On the other hand, a longer story often has a clear beginning, middle, and end. For example, in Richard Connell's "The Most Dangerous Game," the first three scenes maneuver the protagonist, hunter Sanger Rainsford, onto a remote island controlled by a madman who hunts human beings. The middle of the story details Rainsford's attempts to keep from being killed. The ending dramatizes the final clash between the two men, both of whom are hunter and hunted. Each section is clearly demarcated by scene breaks. Most of the action occurs in the middle.

In a novel, the middle may easily be most of the book. By the end of chapter six of *Gone With the Wind*, we have met the four major characters, we know what each wants from the others, we understand the obstacles to getting what they want, and we have witnessed the beginning of the Civil War. The climax takes up only the last chapter. Chapters seven through sixty-two—which is 86 percent of the book—might therefore be called "the middle."

The middle, then, is an enormously important part of your story, even if the term is more amorphous than *beginning* or *end*. Its function, too, is both important and harder to define. Up to this point, the definition we've used is this: *The function of the middle is to develop the implicit promise made by a story's beginning.*

Now, that sounds straightforward enough. If the promise was *Read this and be amused,* then surely the function of the middle is to be amusing. If the promise was *Read this to experience exciting lives you wish you led,* then the function of the middle would seem to be to show us these thrill-packed lives. However, the trouble with that definition isn't that it's false (it's true), but that it doesn't offer much help to the writer. Be amusing *how?* Show us exciting lives *how?* We need more definition.

Try this one: *The middle of a story develops the story's implicit promise by dramatizing incidents that increase conflict, reveal character, and put in place all the various forces that will collide at the story's climax.* In other words, the middle is a bridge—sometimes a long, winding bridge, sometimes a short, direct one. At one end of the bridge, the story's beginning introduces characters, conflict, and (sometimes) symbols. Then in the middle, these same characters, conflicts, and (sometimes) symbols move across the bridge, grouping themselves as they go into alliances and oppositions. Some people change during their journey across the bridge; some don't. Conflicts deepen. People become more emotional. The stakes may rise. By the time the characters reach the other end of the bridge, the forces determining their behavior are clear. At the far end of the bridge, these same forces will collide (the story's climax).

Unity in fiction depends on keeping everybody on the bridge. The forces developed in the middle must emerge naturally out of the characters and situation introduced at the beginning. In turn, the ending must make use of those same forces and conflicts, with nothing important left out and nothing new appearing at the last minute.

Our definition states that the middle develops the implicit promise by "dramatizing incidents." Which specific incidents you dramatize depends, of course, on the story you want to tell. However, guidelines exist to help you pick those incidents that will build on your beginning and propel you toward your ending.

Start by asking yourself three questions important to keeping the story on track.

WHAT *IS* THE TRACK? THREE VITAL DECISIONS

The overall direction of your story is determined by your answers to three crucial questions:

- Whose story is this?
- Who is the point-of-view character?
- What is the throughline?

The answers help you define which scenes you need to write, in what order, and to what end. Once you've made these three choices, writing the middle becomes much easier.

Whose Story Is This?

Your short story or novel will undoubtedly have more than one important character. Ideally readers will be passionately interested in the fate of all your major characters. Even so, in most stories one character commands the most attention. This is the character we automatically think of when we recall the book, the character whose eventual fate defines the book's plot and its meaning. In *Gone With the Wind,* for example, we are very interested in Rhett and Ashley and Melanie, and each represents an important aspect of the antebellum South, but the main story is nonetheless Scarlett O'Hara's. In the same way, *The Great Gatsby* is Jay Gatsby's story, and *Bonfire of the Vanities* is Sherman McCoy's.

Whose story are you writing? The answer will guide your plot, because whoever's story it is will determine your throughline (which we'll discuss below). Consider, for instance, our old friends Jane, Sam, and Martha. Do you want the story to be mostly Jane's, which might be the story of a distraught mother with deep flaws of her own, fighting to save her daughter from messing up both of their lives? Or would you rather write Sam's story, the tale of a man who's spent his whole life evading emotional responsibility only to come to a point where he can't evade any longer? Or maybe you'd rather tell Martha's story. This one could be of a young girl struggling to free herself from toxic parents, making equally toxic choices along the way. Whichever you choose, the other two characters will be important to the story—but subordinate in how you write it.

Who Is the Point-of-View Character?

You have several choices here. In a novel, you can make Sam, Jane, and Martha all point-of-view characters, as long as you stick to one point of view per scene. Or you can write the whole novel from just one point of view, as *The Great Gatsby* is written from the point of view of Nick Carraway. In a short story, it's common to choose just one point-of-view character. All action is then witnessed through the eyes of this character. We readers see only what he sees, know only what he knows, are present only in scenes in which he is present.

The choice of a point-of-view character is thus crucial to how you tell your story. It determines which scenes you can include. If, for instance, your novel is going to be a single point of view through Jane's eyes, you can't include the scene in which Martha leaves the house to catch a bus to Memphis. Jane doesn't know Martha is leaving, so we can't know it either—not until Jane somehow finds out. Although this sounds restricting—and it is—it's also a help in writing the middle of your book. It tells you what you must leave out, and therefore helps you focus on what you must put in. If Jane doesn't see Martha leave, how does she discover that her daughter's gone? How does she react? That's a scene for the middle of your story, plus a direction from which to write it.

It may seem odd to discuss choice of point-of-view character in a section addressing "middles" rather than "beginnings." After all, in a single-point-of-view story, haven't you committed yourself to a choice of point of view by the end of the first paragraph or two? Yes. You have. But I include point of view in "middles" precisely to make the point that just because you wrote the first few scenes doesn't mean you have the right point of view.

Ideally first drafts of the first few scenes are experimental, letting the writer play with his idea, allowing for discovery through the act of putting words on paper. The story takes shape in your mind through the act of writing itself. Additional possibilities occur to you. Other slants present themselves at the edges of your consciousness. If you've rigidly committed to a point of view, you may not be sufficiently open to these surges of imagination. Let them come; let the story shift in your mind. "How do I know what I think," said E.M. Forster, "until I see what I say?"

After you've written a beginning—which we've defined as only two scenes—you'll know more than you did when you first sat down at your desk. This is the time to seriously choose a point-of-view character. You can always rewrite those first two scenes to change point of view, if you have to. Better that than to cut off the possibility of a sudden brainstorm that might improve the story.

After two scenes, however, you've reached the middle. Now you should commit to a point of view. Middles are serious stuff.

But who should that point-of-view character be? Often it's the person whose story you're telling. In a short story about Terry's coming of age, Terry will probably be both protagonist and point of view. But sometimes you gain depth of viewpoint by separating protagonist and point-of-view character. In William Faulkner's classic short story "A Rose for Emily," the main character is Miss Emily Grierson, but the story is narrated by one of the townspeople who observes and judges her desperate life. Similarly, Jay Gatsby's story is told from the point of view of Nick Carraway, who barely knows Gatsby.

Several circumstances prompt the choice of someone other than the protagonist as point-of-view character. If the protagonist dies during the story, as Jay Gatsby does, he's not a good candidate for sole point of view. If the protagonist is insane, as Emily is, you may not want to create the world from inside a mad person's head. If the protagonist knows information you don't want the reader to learn until the end, as in many crime stories, you need to choose a point-of-view character who doesn't know that information. Finally, if the protagonist is not going to change in any significant way—and again, this describes Jay Gatsby—you may want to choose a point-of-view character who *can* change. This brings us to the third question.

What Is the Throughline?

Throughline is a term borrowed from films. It means the main plotline of your story, the one that answers the question, "What happens to the protagonist?" Many, many things may happen to her—as well as to everybody else in the book—but the primary events of the most significant line of action is the throughline. It's what keeps your reader reading.

Thus, in *Bonfire of the Vanities,* the throughline is something like, "This rich, arrogant guy hits a black kid with his Mercedes and everyone else exploits the media circus that the legal case becomes." There are subplots in the book—romances, parent-child relationships, social climbing—but the throughline remains the legal case against Sherman McCoy.

Getting a clear handle on your throughline can make the middle of your book easier to write. It helps you determine which scenes to emphasize. You may write one scene connected with a subplot, or even two, but if you have your throughline firmly in mind, you won't write more than two without returning to it. Some writers write the throughline of their novel on a 3" × 5" card, compressing it to one or two sentences, to make sure it's clear in their minds. Others even tack it above their desks.

In a short story, the throughline is apt to be quieter and less eventful than in a novel. One way to determine the throughline is to ask yourself, "What will be different at the end of this short story from the beginning?" Maybe your character will learn something she didn't know, in which case the throughline might be, "Jane discovers that even though her marriage isn't perfect, she loves her husband enough to live with his faults." Maybe your character will watch someone else's life self-destruct and make a decision to change something about his own. Maybe your character will solve some problem that you present at the beginning of the story.

Whatever your throughline, knowing it in advance can help you keep your story on track. You might not yet know which scenes you will write, but at least you know the end you're writing toward.

But what if you don't? Is it possible to write a short story or novel without determining your throughline—by just setting off to write without a destination, like a guy driving Route 66 in a road movie? Yes, of course it's possible. Many writers start a story because the character or setting or situation intrigues them, and then just write along, interested in seeing what occurs to those chambers along the way. Some writers work this way occasionally (I'm one of them). Some prefer this way. Some can't work any other way.

If you do this, everything I've said about determining your throughline still applies—but not until the second draft. For your first draft, you write unfettered. For your second draft, you determine your throughline and then decide which material you have is still usable. Typically you'll be able to keep more of the later scenes, after you've decided on an ending. The whole first half of the story—or more—may have to be thrown out and replaced with scenes that actually fit with your later decisions about character, plot, and ending. So long as you determine your throughline at some point, it doesn't really matter to the work where you do it. (Although it may matter to *you*. More on this when we discuss outlining.)

MOVING ALONG THE TRACK: THINKING IN SCENES

Now you know your protagonist, your point-of-view character and your throughline. Next comes deciding which scenes to write.

Notice that I said, "deciding which scenes to write" rather than "deciding what happens in the story." Plot is usually described in terms of things that happen, but the problem with this is that "things that happen" can in turn be described in exposition. A plot summary tells what happened in a story. You are not writing a plot summary. You're writing fiction, and fiction occurs in scenes. For that reason, it's helpful to think about structuring the middle of your book in terms of scenes, not events. An event may take more than one scene, may take one scene exactly, half a scene, or no scenes at all. These are decisions you can make before you begin the middle of your story. Start by listing the events.

Consider, for example, that rewrite of "Cinderella." Here's a chronological list of events that occur in that story:

1. A man has a wife and a daughter.
2. The wife dies.
3. After a time the man remarries a disagreeable woman with two daughters of her own.
4. The stepmother and stepsisters treat Cinderella badly.
5. The father dies.
6. The stepmother and stepsisters treat Cinderella even worse.
7. The king is distressed because his only son isn't married.
8. The king decides to hold a ball and invite all the kingdom's eligible young women.
9. Etc.

In your version of "Cinderella," you probably won't apportion one scene to each of these events. The traditional version, for instance, allows no dramatized scenes for events one through three, instead summarizing them in exposition ("Once upon a time there was a man with a beloved wife and cherished daughter. The wife died, leaving the man a widow. After a time he remarried …"). On the other hand, event six is interesting and important enough that you might give it three scenes: Cinderella forced to wait on her stepsisters, Cinderella ridiculed and called names, Cinderella sent to sleep among the ashes. You'll have to make a decision on event five, the father's death—dramatize the deathbed scene and Cinderella's grief, or just mention both in a brief expository paragraph?

You can see from this the difference between an event and a scene. The process works the same for your story: First, guided by your throughline, list *all* the events that happen to all the characters from the beginning until the end. (If you don't yet have a throughline, list events as far into the story as you can; you can always repeat this part after the throughline becomes clearer to you.) If events are going on simultaneously in different places, list them in arbitrary sequence and bracket them. At this stage, throw in every event you can think of that's interesting and relevant.

Now go through and cross out those that aren't happening in the presence of any of your point-of-view characters. You must find another way to let us know about these. Add any scenes necessary to this discovery. For instance, if Sam and his secretary Gina are having an affair but the only point-of-view character is Sam's wife, Jane, cross out the scene that reads "Sam and Gina go to a motel." Figure out how and when Jane discovers this, and in the appropriate place in the list add, "Jane walks in on Sam and Gina," or "Jane's mother phones to tell her about Sam's affair," or "Jane hires a private detective," or "Sam tells Jane about Gina," or "Gina spitefully phones Jane about her affair with Sam." Which you choose will, of course, depend on the personalities you've created for these people.

Now you have a list of story events, adjusted for point of view. Take the time to think about each one. Is it important and interesting enough to dramatize in a full scene? Might it need two scenes? Would it be better to just summarize it in exposition?

The scenes you spend the most time on should be those that relate directly to your throughline. In addition, which scenes you dramatize most fully will inevitably be a function of what you find most interesting. Your choices become one component of your individual style, which emerges partly from what you choose to say and partly from how you say it. Don't try to direct this process too much. If a scene interests you, write it. If, later on, it seems mostly irrelevant, you can always cut it in the second draft.

If your list was a partial one, maybe comprising only three or four scenes, don't worry about it. Write those scenes, and when they're exhausted, make a second list of subsequent events and scenes. Maybe by that time you'll know what your throughline is.

You can often dramatically improve a short story idea by trying for the fewest possible scenes that will still tell the story. Many beginners' stories are padded with unnecessary scenes. Study your scene list, trying to eliminate scenes or combine scenes. (Could Jane learn about Sam's affair at the same time she's searching frantically for Martha?) I've frequently been startled by how much a story can be sharpened by concentrating its events and emotions into the bare minimum of scenes. You can achieve this by cutting after the story is written, but it's better to build in economy and speed in the first place.

Is this process an outline? Yes and no. Outlines scare some writers. They feel that if they have an outline, they're straitjacketed into a certain set of maneuvers, and they resent that (even when it's their own outline. Nobody said writing was logical.). These writers need space in their first drafts. They have a broad idea of the plot of a book but don't really know what they're going to say until they say it. For such writers, the structure only emerges as they create, which means two things: Their first drafts are a mess, and only in the second draft do they think about design and pattern.

Other writers love outlines. They like to have the shape of a book firmly in mind before they start. They make notes, chapter by chapter. They work out all variations of point of view. They detail the narrative design. Orson Scott Card, for instance, thought in minute detail for two years about his novel *Ender's Game*. Then he sat down and wrote it, nonstop, in two weeks. This is an extreme example—but not an isolated one.

If you want to think of this event/point-of-view/scene list as an outline, go ahead. However, its provisional and partial nature makes it more flexible than a traditional outline. So if you want to think of it as just a few notes jotted down on scrap paper to guide you through the middle of the story (which is how *I* think of it), feel free.

PLANNING FOR THE CLIMAX:
NOVELS VERSUS SHORT STORIES

In the midst of all this guided flexibility, however, you *must* dramatize one scene in your novel: the climax. You have no choice about this. A climax that occurs offstage is frustrating and disappointing to novel readers (short stories work differently; we'll come to them in a minute). Nor should the climax speed by in a few paragraphs. This is the point you've been building toward for three hundred pages; the reader, who's also invested three hundred pages' worth of reading time, wants to witness the payoff in person and at sufficiently satisfying length.

The climax properly belongs to a story's ending, and we'll discuss it more thoroughly in chapter seven. The point here is that while you make your list of events and scenes, this is one scene to star.

How do you know which scene is the climax? The climax is the culmination of your throughline, the event that brings into collision all the forces you've set up. The climax is the point where something has to give—and does.

One way to determine the climax is to ask yourself how a reader would answer the question, "How does this book end?" The answer might not be the actual ending. *The Great Gatsby,* for instance, ends with Nick Carraway's decision to return to the Midwest. Before that comes Gatsby's pathetic funeral. But if you ask a nonscholarly reader, "How does *Gatsby* end?" he's likely to say, "Daisy runs over Myrtle, only Myrtle's husband thinks Gatsby is driving, and then he shoots Gatsby." The climax here is the confusion over who's in the driver's seat (literally and symbolically), and Fitzgerald spends sufficient time on it: More than 25 percent of the page count details that last trip to New York and its immediate aftermath.

In a novel, then, it's important to identify the moment when all the forces in your story come together to produce emotional and thematic fireworks. Although that moment comes near the end of the story, you plan for it in the middle. After mentally identifying those forces, you can work backward, choosing scenes for the middle that will dramatize the inexorable build of conflicting elements.

Consider an example: *Jurassic Park,* which we've examined before. All of the following forces collide at the climax: (1) the greed and hubris of the corporation building a theme park devoted to cloned dinosaurs; greed and hubris have led the park engineers into dangerous secrecy and equally dangerous cost-cutting; (2) human error, even on the part of the best-intentioned members of the project team; (3) the duplicity of a key data-systems employee; (4) the limitations of even the most sophisticated computer programs; and (5) the endless adaptive resources of nature, which humanity consistently underestimates.

All of these forces are dramatized repeatedly in the middle. We are shown instances of corporate hubris ("Nothing can go wrong. This is fail-safe."). We are shown engineers and builders cutting corners. We are shown an employee selling corporate secrets. We are shown the computer failing to recognize crucial events because it wasn't programmed to look for them. We are shown one breed of dinosaur that is more intelligent and fierce than its creators expected, and another that breeds even though biological theory has declared that impossible.

Because we are shown all these things in the middle of the novel, we're well prepared for the ending. We can see from Crichton's careful dramatizations that this situation is a disaster waiting to happen. And we're intensely curious about *how* the disaster will occur, and when, and to whom. The middle has done its job by maneuvering all the forces into place for an explosive climax.

A traditionally plotted short story also may have this classic kind of action climax, followed by a tidying up of loose ends (the denouement). In many contemporary short stories, however, the climax works a little differently. Often the point is the change a character undergoes, or a realization she comes to, and it's difficult to pinpoint the exact moment it occurs. Everything in the story contributes to the change, and then the change or realization itself may be indicated by only a sentence or two.

For example, in Raymond Carver's story "Fat," whose opening we looked at earlier, the entire story is taken up by the waitress's serving the fat man, arguing about him with her coworkers, going home with her insensitive husband, and telling the story afterward to her friend Rita. Then the story concludes with the lines:

> It is August.
> My life is going to change. I feel it.

That's it: the climax. Obviously Carver didn't spend a lot of time dramatizing his protagonist's realization of change. Instead he spends the time carefully detailing events that make the change understandable to us, the readers. He *shows* us all the reasons the narrator has for being dissatisfied with her life: her co-workers' narrow-mindedness and insensitivity, the indifference of her husband to anything she tells him, Rita's incomprehension. We're prepared for the three-sentence climax because we can see that the waitress's life *ought* to change. No elaborate explanation is necessary.

Many short stories use this structure, and if you write such a short story, your climax may also occur in a few understated sentences. To succeed, however, it must be backed by middle scenes that *have* been dramatized, and dramatized so well that they illuminate the character change. We should think, "Well, yes, given what he's been through, he might very well feel that way at the end." For this kind of short story, preparation for the understated climax makes the difference between success and failure. That preparation occurs in the scenes you write in the middle.

MAKING SURE THE READER STAYS ON TRACK: FORMAL STRUCTURAL DESIGNS

In a short story, it's usually not difficult to make sure a reader doesn't become confused. A short story has room for only a handful of events.

Most are narrated in chronological order. Usually there aren't more than three or four important characters to keep track of. As long as you provide sufficient transition phrases ("Two weeks later …" "It had been different back in college …"), nobody gets lost.

A novel is a different proposition. Some resemble short stories in their straightforward narration and relatively few characters. Others, however, require that the reader keep straight dozens of characters, multiple flashbacks, shifts in location, and changes in point of view. A reader who puts the book down for a while—say, to get a sandwich—can become disoriented.

Formal structural designs are one way to prevent that. A *formal structural design* is an overall plan for presenting scenes throughout an entire novel. It doesn't dictate the content of those scenes, but it does provide a pattern for presenting them. Like the pattern of the tides, it helps the reader anticipate the ebb and flow of narrative, leaving her free to concentrate on the fascinating revelations periodically uncovered.

It also helps the writer. Faced with what seems like a cast of thousands and globe-spanning shifts in locale, you can use a structural design to help decide which scene goes where—an immense help in writing the middle of a complex novel. Four common structural designs are straight chronological, regularly recurring viewpoints, multiviewpoint chronological sections, and parallel running scenes. Each has advantages and disadvantages.

A straight chronological structure is the easiest to follow (and to write). You start at the beginning of the story and show us each major event in the order either that it happened to your protagonist or that your protagonist learned about it. There may or may not be brief flashbacks, but they don't last long enough to distract the reader from the main plot. When you get to the last important event, you stop writing. A classic example of the straight chronological structure is *David Copperfield*. As it happens to David, so does it happen to the reader, throughout roughly thirty years.

The advantages of the straight chronological structure are clarity and consistency. No reader can get lost, because there are no large jumps in time or point of view. Consistency is guaranteed because we are asked to absorb only one person's reactions to story events.

The limitations of a straight chronological structure are point of view and range. Since this structure works best with a single point of view, whenever the point-of-view character isn't present, you can't show us what's happening to anybody else. Similarly, if you've led a reader to expect that he's seeing events in the order they happened, your emotional range is limited to what you can wring out of that order. You can't leave out an emotionally tense scene and include it later, out of chronological sequence, just because it has more impact later. If you do, the reader will feel that you cheated. You set up the expectation that we're seeing the story as it unfolds; you must deliver on that implicit promise.

Suppose you have two or more point-of-view characters. Can you still get a sense of consistency and clarity? Yes. One way is to set up a pattern of *regularly recurring viewpoints* so that the reader comes to expect to hear from each character in the same order.

For example, Bradley Denton's novel *Buddy Holly Is Alive and Well on Ganymede* has six point-of-view characters. Each chapter opens with a section in the point of view of Oliver Vale, the protagonist. Next comes a shorter section in the point of view of Sharon Sharpston, Oliver's psychiatrist. Then come two or more short sections divided among the remaining four points of view. This keeps the novel, a complex postmodern fantasy, from becoming confusing, even when different events happen simultaneously to different characters.

It also creates a sense of anticipation in the reader: "What will Sharon have to say about *that* development!" Finally, the carefully recurring order subtly reassures the reader than even in a story as wildly imaginative as *Buddy Holly*, the author has everything under control. There's a design here. It will all come together in the end (which it does).

A disadvantage of regularly recurring viewpoints is that they may come to seem too mechanical. In addition, you may find yourself having to perform procrustean operations on your story to make it fit the point-of-view pattern. Minor variations are possible (in two chapters of Denton's book, we don't hear from Sharon at all), but if you find yourself inventing peripheral events or characters just because "it's their turn," this design is not good for your novel.

So, what to do if you have multiple points of view but don't want to rotate them regularly? Maybe you only need a certain point-of-view character twice during the whole novel—but you *do* need him then. Or maybe you don't want to be straitjacketed by a regularly recurring order because in some parts of the book it will create more tension to have Jane's scene come before Sam's, but other parts of the book will be sharper if Sam's scene comes first, followed by Martha's, and then Jane's. However, you don't want the appearance of complete capriciousness as you switch points of view. You want some structure.

I was faced with this problem in my fourth novel, *An Alien Light*, which uses six point-of-view characters, each with very lengthy scenes, many of them occurring simultaneously in different settings. I found this very difficult to write. By the time I'd worked through five characters, even I had forgotten what I'd left the sixth one doing. And the reader had probably forgotten which complicated events occurred before other events, after others, or simultaneously.

My solution was the *multiviewpoint chronological section*. All this jawbreaker of a word means is that you break the novel into clearly labeled parts. Each part covers a set period of time, and everything that happens in that period is in that section, no matter whom it happens to or whose eyes we view it through. Within each section I put several chapters of varying lengths. Each chapter contained one and only one point of view. Thus the reader quickly picked up my signals that every time a new chapter started, the point of view had changed; every time a new part of the novel started (there are seven parts), the story had finished with the previous time or place and everybody got to start fresh. The book is still complicated (it involves three separate cultures), but the structure I imposed on it gives the reader a fighting chance of knowing where he is, when, and with whom. Noah Gordon used the same design in his medical novel *The Death Committee,* in which the sections are clearly labeled "Summer," "Fall and Winter," and "Spring and Summer, The Full Circle."

Multiviewpoint chronological sections offer the advantage of greater flexibility within each section. Scenes can be ordered to build tension, withhold information from the reader, or contrast behaviors. However, because the structure resides in the divisions rather than in the content, this design is inherently weaker than the others and so does not provide the reader with as much sense of rhythm, anticipation, or inevitability. The sections may not all be the same length; the same point-of-view characters may not turn up in each section. There aren't patterns to count on.

Maximum rhythm and anticipation, in contrast, are achieved by using *parallel running scenes.* In this structure, two stories are going on simultaneously, alternating with each other chapter by chapter, until they come together at the end. An example is Ursula K. Le Guin's fine novel of anarchy as a viable political system, *The Dispossessed.* Chapters one, three, five, seven, nine, and eleven tell the "real" story, with the main conflict. Chapters two, four, six, eight, ten, and twelve are sequential flashbacks covering the life of the protagonist, Shevek, from birth until the point where chapter one begins. They show how Shevek became a person who could get involved in this particular conflict, in this particular way. Chapter thirteen resolves everything.

Obviously, such a structure risks tremendous pitfalls. Le Guin's story is much more fragmented than if she had told it in straight chronological sequence. What she loses in clarity, however, she gains in thematic richness: The chapters dealing with Shevek's past comment on and contrast with the "story-time" chapters flanking them. In addition, her careful balancing of past and present illuminates Shevek's career: He is a temporal physicist, dealing in the ambiguities of time. I think the novel gains more than it loses by its elaborate structure. Some critics, however, have found Le Guin's structure too self-conscious and contrived.

A simpler version of parallel running scenes balances not time but setting. Some romances, for example, alternate chapters in which the heroine has adventures in one place while the hero has them in another, until the adventures bring them together. This, too, can seem fragmented, or it can build anticipation and inevitability, depending both on what the story events are and on how well they're fitted to the parallel structure. As with all other choices in writing, there are both gains and losses to this design.

CHOOSING A STRUCTURAL DESIGN

How do you choose the best structural design for your novel? As with your throughline, you have two choices. You can plan the whole book ahead of time to fit a chosen design. Or you can write it however it occurs to you, read your first draft, choose the design that best shapes the existing material, and rewrite as necessary.

Both methods can work. The point is that the final design should not be haphazard. By considering the options open to you, you can make an informed choice. Your best design is one that will keep your reader on track—and also make it easier for you to write the middle part of your book.

There's another important aspect to planning and writing the middle of your short story or novel: character development. In fact, it's important enough to deserve a chapter of its own.

EXERCISES FOR MIDDLES

1. Choose three novels you know well. For each, summarize the throughline in a sentence or two. If you can't do this, reread the section of this chapter called "What Is the Throughline?" (Remember, throughlines deal with plot, not theme.) Summarize the throughlines of three short stories as well.

2. For one of the above novels and one of the short stories, make a list of all the forces developed in the middle. How does each contribute to the climax?

3. Pick one of the short stories and list the scenes (a longish story works best for this). Now consider each scene separately. What is its function—to develop character, advance plot, or both? How does the scene contribute to the throughline? If you feel ambitious, do this for a short novel.

4. Pull out one of your own finished stories. Summarize its throughline. List the scenes. How does each advance plot, develop character, contribute to the throughline? Try to find two scenes you could combine; how would you do it? Try to find one scene you could cut; how would you keep in the story any vital information the scene contains? Does it seem to you that this story could have used any additional scenes? Where? Why?

5. Look again at your story. Try to imagine it from the point of view of a secondary character. Is it more or less interesting? If this exercise intrigues you, read Valerie Martin's novel *Mary Reilly,* a retelling of Robert Louis Stevenson's *Strange Case of Dr. Jekyll*

and Mr. Hyde from the point of view of Dr. Jekyll's housemaid; Jean Rhys's *Wide Sargasso Sea,* a retelling *of Jane Eyre* from the point of view of the first Mrs. Rochester; or Tanith Lee's *Red As Blood,* a retelling of many Grimm fairy tales from unexpected points of view.

6. Choose a favorite multiviewpoint novel. Analyze how, and how often, the author changes points of view. (It can be helpful to mark all the point-of-view changes in the margin.) How does the author mark transitions from one point of view to another? Do the switches follow any pattern? Is there anything here applicable to your novel?

CHAPTER 5

UNDER DEVELOPMENT: YOUR CHARACTERS AT MIDSTORY

Your character is having a midlife crisis. His life exists in your story, and midway through your page count he is supposed to undergo a significant change. He sees the error of his ways or he is made wise by experience or he has a religious conversion or he simply grows up. By the end of the story he will behave much differently than he did at the beginning. He will be a different person—while, of course, remaining the *same* person the reader has come to know.

How do you pull off that one?

It's not always easy. The danger is that the character's change of heart will seem arbitrary and unmotivated. Sam has been behaving like an evasive husband and father for two hundred pages, and then suddenly he "comes to realize" that his family is the most important thing in the world to him and he moves back home, listens attentively to Jane, and takes Martha to ball games. Jane and Martha are bewildered, but not nearly as bewildered as the reader, who is likely to think, "Huh? *Sam?* Give me a break! I don't believe it for a minute!"

And yet writers do create convincing character changes all the time. Elizabeth Bennet, in Jane Austen's *Pride and Prejudice,* starts out by disliking Mr. Darcy and ends up in love with him (a change still used by romance writers). W. Somerset Maugham's Philip Carey begins *Of Human Bondage* ashamed of his physical deformity, defenseless against his own emotions, conventional in his beliefs, and something of a snob. Five hundred sixty-five pages later, Philip has made his peace with his lameness, gained at least some control over his passions, tested his beliefs against the world, and now is preparing to marry the uneducated daughter of a penniless clerk. Even a short story allows for at least the beginning of a genuine character change, as we have already seen in Carver's "Fat."

To make character changes convincing, four things must happen (we'll look at each in detail in this chapter):

- The reader must understand your character's initial personality, and especially her motivation: *why* she's behaving the way she is.

- The reader must see evidence that your character is capable of change (not everyone is).

- The reader must see dramatized a pattern of experiences that might reasonably be expected to affect someone.

- The reader must see a plausible new motivation replace the character's old motivation.

The first three of these should occur mostly in the middle of your story (the fourth may also occur there). If you take care to set up character changes in the middle, such changes won't seem arbitrary or contrived at the end. In addition, if you maintain control over your character's motivation, you will automatically enhance other story elements: plot, tension, and theme. This is because *stories grow out of what characters do, and, in turn, what characters do grows out of what they want.*

A READER'S VIEW: TWO KINDS OF MOTIVATION

As anyone who reads a newspaper already knows, human beings are capable of anything. Something motivates those people who collect

Victorian underwear, leave eight million dollars to their cat, commit axe murders, risk their lives for strangers, or tap-dance the length of California. In journalism, it's sufficient to let the subject himself answer the question, "Why did you do it?" Making the action itself credible isn't an issue; it *happened*. In fiction, however, it didn't happen (by definition), and not all actions will strike your reader as equally plausible. Therefore, it makes sense to consider character motivation not only in terms of the character himself (he's angry, he's in love, he wants to get even), but also in terms of the reader. Reader understanding is the key to creating credible motivation for your protagonist.

Looked at this way, there are two kinds of character motivation. Each dictates a different writing strategy.

First are motives that are easily understandable to the reader because she would feel the same way in a similar situation. You, the writer, don't have to work too hard at this kind of motivation. Readers will readily understand why a mother risks danger to save her baby, why a detective wants to solve a crime, why a woman who just lost her fiancé to her sister doesn't choose to attend their wedding. In such situations, all you need is a brief confirmation that the characters are what we expect, and we'll accept their actions. Show us briefly that the mother loves her baby, the detective is a conscientious guy, the jilted sister feels hurt. A paragraph or two will often do it.

The writer's task is much more complicated when motivation is counter to our expectations of the world. Some of the best stories have characters with motives that are more interesting—because less predictable—than the ones cited above. However, the less common the character's motive, and the more it violates our stereotypes, the more background information you'll have to supply to make us understand why this person is doing what he's doing.

Consider, for example, that jilted sister. Suppose she doesn't refuse to attend the wedding. Suppose instead she actually seems pleased that her fiancé was starting to pay so much attention to her sister. Suppose she makes excuses to leave them alone together, praises them lavishly to each other, seems to *want* them to flirt and touch. Why might she do all that?

There are several possible reasons. Maybe she's come to realize that she made a mistake, this isn't the man for her, and she's hoping that if he falls for Sissy the whole awful situation can be resolved without anyone's getting hurt.

Or maybe her motive is more sinister: She needs to hold power over everybody around her, and being the ostensible victim in a love triangle based on guilt will give her plenty of secret power over both her sister *and* her husband.

Or maybe she's always felt a devastating inferiority to her sister. Now she helplessly believes there's no way she could ever compete with such a goddess as Sissy, so the best way to remain a part of both her fiancé's and her sister's lives is to go along with their attraction for each other.

Or maybe …

All these reactions are certainly possible to human nature. None, however, will be your reader's automatic assumption of how a jilted woman feels or behaves. Therefore, you will have to work much harder to make her motivation clear and credible. You might show us her private thoughts. You might let us hear her candidly discuss the situation with her friend, her dog, or her therapist. You might let us see her behave in similar fashion—with kindness or with deviousness or with low self-esteem—in other unrelated situations. Probably you'll need to do all these things, because when an initial motivation is out of the ordinary, only a pattern of incidents in the middle of the story will convince us that it's genuine.

Beginning writers often have trouble with this. At the end of the story, when it turns out that it was Jane who first gave her daughter drugs, the amazed reader says, "Jane? Martha's own mother? Why would a mother do *that?*"

The writer answers, "Because she's jealous that her daughter still has all her life ahead of her, while Jane's life is such a mess."

"But," the reader says, "you never said Jane was so jealous of Martha!"

"Yes, I did," the writer answers indignantly, "right here on page sixty-eight!"

Unfortunately one mention on page sixty-eight isn't going to do it. A mother who supplies her daughter with drugs out of jealousy is so far out of most readers' expectations that to make this credible you'd need an extensive pattern of incidents. You would have to show us Jane jealous of Martha's freedom to drop a boyfriend (much easier than dropping husband Sam); Jane reacting spitefully to Martha's getting a fun job (Jane hates her job); Jane showing willful negligence for other people (maybe she leaves a hit-and-run accident); Jane unable to control her own destructive impulses; Jane trying on Martha's clothes, wrapped in despair because they don't fit her aging body; Jane telling her best friend she never wanted to be a mother at all. After all that, we might believe Jane is capable of supplying Martha with drugs out of jealousy. We won't like Jane, but we'll understand her.

This is one of fiction's major challenges: making readers understand a character's motives when those motives are not simple. The way you create such understanding is through patterns of incidents. No one occurrence will be enough. However, it's worth the effort, because complex motivations lead to unexpected actions, and such actions create interesting plots.

In a short story, of course, you don't have as much room to dramatize as many incidents. However, you still must show more than one motivating incident to make a character change believable. In "Fat," for instance, Carver includes three different sets of responses to the fat man: from the narrator's coworkers, from her husband, and from her friend, Rita. None of them understands what the narrator is trying to say. There is a *pattern* of incomprehension that causes the narrator to think she must change her life—all presented in six pages.

The shorter the piece of fiction, the more skillful you must be in your choice of incidents. That's why there are more good novelists than good short story writers.

What does all this mean in terms of planning the middle of your story? It means that when you list events to turn into scenes, you must include events that will make clear *why* your characters are doing what they're doing.

For instance, a common type of story conflict arises when a character wants two mutually exclusive things. This happens to all of us every day: We want to go to the Wednesday late-night party *and* be fresh for work the next day. We want to lose ten pounds *and* eat linzer torte. More seriously, we want justice for all but only if we don't have to personally give up anything to get it, freedom to do what we want but only if other people behave the way we think they should. "The problems of the human heart in conflict with itself—that alone can make good writing," said William Faulkner.

When your character wants two conflicting things, or acts out of two conflicting motives, you must develop both in the middle part of your story. This means including on your scene list incidents that will dramatize both. If, for instance, Jane is torn between her savage jealousy of Martha and her more maternal love, the jealousy scenes need to be balanced by scenes of Jane at least trying to express her concern for Martha. Both kinds of scenes will need to be strongly written if we're going to believe Jane's internal conflict.

In a short story, especially, these same scenes must do double duty: They must also advance the main plot. This means you need to give thought to choosing scenes in which your characters not only *do* something, but also do that something in a way that is revealing of their personalities. In a novel, most of the scenes will also meet these twin goals, although at novel length you have some room for purely characterizing flashbacks and digressions.

SHOWING THAT CHARACTERS ARE CAPABLE OF CHANGE

If your character changes significantly during the course of your story, we need to believe that she's among those human beings capable of change. We've all known people who are so rigid in their beliefs or behavior that they'll never change. They're locked into views of the world they acquired at some earlier stage of life, and it's useless to present them with any other ideas. They don't hear them, even though they may appear to be listening. They can't hear. They have too much invested in their current world views, and it would be too threatening to be wrong. Your character, however, isn't like that. He's capable of learning from experience.

How do you make us believe that? By showing him doing it.

If, for instance, Sam is an evasive and unemotional father but capable of seeing his own deficiencies once the level of crisis is high enough, then you show Sam doing just that in some different, unrelated crisis earlier in the book. Maybe you give us a flashback to Sam's days in Vietnam. He remained aloof from the men in his platoon, acting as if he weren't actually there (because he wished he weren't). Some crisis on a dangerous reconnaissance, however, forced him into emotionally risky affiliation with someone else, and Sam rose to the occasion. You give us this in a flashback. This flashback both helps us understand Sam better *and* prepares us for his eventual reconnection with his daughter—after Martha's behavior has become desperate enough.

Or maybe a war scene wouldn't fit with the tone of your novel. So instead you show us Sam in a more domestic crisis, perhaps involving his aging mother, who has to move into a nursing home. When the situation is heated enough, Sam comes through. Not before, and not happily—but he does come through.

Even small parts of scenes can foreshadow your character's ability to become whatever you eventually have him become. Though Elizabeth Bennet dislikes Mr. Darcy for most of *Pride and Prejudice,* we believe her eventual change of heart toward him for two reasons. First, we see that Elizabeth is capable of changing her opinion when there is real evidence: In earlier scenes she revises her opinion of George Wickham, Charles Bingley, and Charlotte Lucas. Second, we see that she has a high regard for behavior that is ethical, generous, and self-effacing. When Darcy behaves in those ways about Elizabeth's sister's disastrous elopement, it's not difficult to accept that his behavior would have an effect on Elizabeth's opinion of him.

Foreshadow your protagonist's major change by (1) showing he's capable of other changes, and (2) showing values he holds that make changing his mind plausible.

WHY DOES THE CHARACTER ACTUALLY CHANGE?

This is the easy part. The character changes because of the events of the plot. You already know those. If you've shown us what the character is like in the beginning, and you've convinced us she's capable of change, the story events will form a pattern that makes change seem inevitable.

The key word here—as it was in complex motivation—is *pattern.* In real life people sometimes undergo real change as a result of one experience, even if the experience seems trivial to outsiders. In fiction, however, unless the single event is a pretty traumatic one, character changes should be the result of repeated, convincing experiences the character is forced to live through.

For example, Martha's first attempt at running away from home probably won't significantly change Sam, her father. If it *did,* his uncommitted fatherhood wouldn't seem sufficiently uncommitted. Instead, Sam tries to rationalize the whole thing:

> All kids ran away from home at least once, Sam thought, picking up the newspaper and raising the sports section between himself and Jane. Running away was normal. Why, he'd done it himself at fourteen, he and Tommy Bannister, although of course then there weren't all these drugs on the street. Still, Jane was overreacting. Just like she always did. Martha had learned her lesson—look at her tear-stained face, for Chrissake—and it wouldn't happen again. Kids just went through stages, was all. Jane should accept that, learn to roll with the punches.... The Pittsburgh Pirates looked very good in spring training.

It will take repeated problems with Martha—your whole novel, in fact—to really force Sam into change.

In a short story, again, you must work faster. The experience that causes change might appear to be a single, small-scale event. In James Purdy's story "The Beard," for example, a seemingly trivial incident—an adult son shows up for a visit home sporting a new beard—causes repercussions that unravel the whole family. Here what makes the changes plausible is not the story event, which is merely a catalyst, but the careful creation of the patterns of family tension. A reader gets the impression that just about anything could have set this family off. They're primed for confrontation. And how is that conveyed? Through a pattern of repeated confrontations, both past and present.

The guideline here is to ask yourself, "Am I presenting the kind of experiences that make the reader think, 'Well, yes, if this event happened to that person, he probably *would* behave like that. I might not, but *he* would.'"

REPLACING AN OLD MOTIVATION WITH A NEW ONE

The outcome of all this dramatization of motive, preparation for change, and depiction of story events is to replace a character's initial motivation with a different one. That is, the character started out wanting one thing and somewhere in the middle switches to wanting something else (which will prepare nicely for the ending). Sam starts out wanting to be left alone, uninvolved in his daughter's problems; he might switch to wanting desperately to rescue Martha from self-destruction. Elizabeth Bennet starts out wanting to promote her sister Jane's happiness and to annoy Mr. Darcy; she switches to wanting to marry Mr. Darcy.

It can be helpful to stop somewhere in the middle of your novel to list these motivation switches on a piece of paper. What did each character want in the beginning of the book? What does he want now? Is it still the same desire? Do you *know?* If you don't, give it some serious thought.

This advice applies to short stories as well as to novels, with the difference that in a short story the change in motivation usually comes at the end, not in the middle. In a short story you may not have the space to show your protagonist acting on his new motive, but he usually at least becomes aware of it at the end. When Carver's unnamed heroine thinks, "My life is going to change. I feel it," that implies a change in motivation, although one whose specifics Carver doesn't choose to explore.

A SPECIAL CASE OF MOTIVATION: VILLAINS

Everybody loves to hate the bad guy. But not all bad guys are created equal. Some arouse a lot more hatred or fear or anger than others. Some villains are chilling enough to cause nightmares; others merely cause yawns. Why?

Your book, of course, may not contain a villain at all, only muddled people living at cross-purposes with each other. But if you do have a villain, he or she will be much more successful if self-justified. Villains that act out of pure unadulterated evil are fun for comic books, but strong adult-fiction villains act out of motives that make sense *to themselves*. Even Hitler was convinced that he had a right to commit his horrendous acts. Show us your villain's self-justification—motives, beliefs, rationalizations—and he will become much more plausible than the stock "bad guy in a black hat."

Consider, for example, Captain Queeg in Herman Wouk's Pulitzer-prize winner, *The Caine Mutiny*. Queeg torments and punishes his crew, finally driving one sailor to a mental breakdown and another usually reasonable officer to mutiny. But Queeg is no power-hungry sadist. Instead he is an inadequate man hopelessly out of his league, who retaliates with petty bullying. The bullying escalates as Queeg himself increasingly loses control. Finally his men just can't stand it anymore. As a villain, Queeg is frightening because he's plausible. Any of us could work for him. And to himself, his appalling actions are fully justified by his panicky need to whip this mine-sweeper crew into military shape.

Sometimes the villain even becomes sympathetic, at least to some degree. Nanike, the protagonist of Nadine Gordimer's "A City of the Dead, A City of the Living," is a black woman living in South Africa. In their small house she and her husband hide an activist, a man with a vision for their apartheid-torn country. At the end of the story Nanike turns the activist in to the police, who will almost certainly torture him. She does so from a complicated mix of jealousy, resentment, and neglect that she herself doesn't really understand. But because we see her harsh daily life, she becomes more to us than just a betrayer. She, too, is a victim of her country's brutal politics.

Less subtly, genre fiction frequently includes a villain: the murderer in mystery novels, the "wrong man" in romances, the space conquerors or exploiters in science fiction, the corporate raider trying to destroy a company in "glitter romances." These antagonists will be both more convincing and more interesting if you let us see how they regard their villainies. The murderer may be motivated by a wrong once done to her. The cad may believe that women are happier being dominated and used. The aliens may be genetically hardwired for violence (or they may just be trying to show us we're their equal—worthy of being fought with). The corporate raider believes that destroying companies is healthy economic Darwinism. Certainly you don't have to convince us of the rightness of the villain's motives (if you do, he becomes the hero)—but do give him motives.

If you don't know why your villain is causing everybody else all this trouble—other than if he didn't, there would be no plot—stop writing. Think about the villain until you do know his psychology and motivation. Your story will be stronger.

An Encouraging Word on Middles

The major function of the middle of a story is to set up the ending—to make it a plausible, satisfying fulfillment of the implicit promise. The middle does this by clearly dramatizing those forces that will collide at the climax, including any potential character changes. If you do this conscientiously in the middle, you will find the ending much easier to write. Middles *are* hard—Dante was right—but they're worth the effort. A middle that does what it's supposed to can make the ending a positive delight to write—and, more important, to read.

MORE EXERCISES FOR MIDDLES

1. Choose a short story or novel you know well, one in which the protagonist undergoes a significant character change. Consider:
    a. What did the character want in the beginning of the story?
    b. What did she want by the end?

c. Which experiences helped change her? List them.

d. How did the author show that the character was even capable of change?

2. Repeat the above exercise for one of your own finished stories. Do you see places where characterization is weak? Could you improve it by adding a scene or by supplementing existing dialogue, thoughts, description, or action?

3. Invent a character who wants something contrary to what readers would ordinarily expect. Write a few pages of interior monologue for this character in which he explains and justifies what he wants, why he should have it, and how he's going about getting it. Try to make him sound convincing and natural.

4. Using the same character, write a two-person conversation in which he tries to persuade another character to join him in whatever he's doing. The other person resists. Try to make both characters' dialogue sound natural. Is there a story idea here?

5. Choose a story in the genre in which you want to write (mystery, literary, mainstream, science fiction, romance, etc.). Pick a story that you recall as having a memorable villain. Reread it. What is the villain's motivation? Is it clear? If so, how is it made clear? If not, would this be a better story if the villain were motivated by something other than pure nastiness? Given the villain's circumstances, what might these motives have been?

CHAPTER 6

HELP FOR MIDDLES: GETTING UNSTUCK

There are writers who find writing middles exciting. These authors feel that the hard part is now out of the way. They've launched their characters; they've charted their plot; they're eager for the fun of midvoyage, skimming along under full sail. Middles, the trade winds of writing, exhilarate them.

I don't know any of these people.

For me, as for many other writers I know, middles represent a genuine psychological problem: We get stuck. We may be stuck for a few days, or a few months, or—as in the case of Harold Brodkey's novel *The Runaway Soul,* thirty years late—a few decades. We may or may not dignify this state with the label "writer's block." Either way, we're stuck. We just can't seem to make ourselves go forward with our novel or short story. Sometimes we can't even make ourselves sit down in the same room with the damn thing.

I have been stuck in the middle of five out of my six novels. What I've learned from those experiences—none of which I'd willingly relive—is that even though being stuck always *feels* the same (frustrating), it isn't always caused by the same thing. There are different kinds of getting stuck—and some of them are even beneficial. There are also different methods of getting yourself unstuck. These methods work.

Common reasons for getting stuck on either a short story or a novel are fear of failure, fear of success, literary fogginess, and wrong direction. In addition, novelists may get stuck if they become overwhelmed by the sheer magnitude of writing a novel: in the page count, the time investment, and the stamina required.

FEAR OF FAILURE: THE TOLSTOY SYNDROME

My 1981 short story "Casey's Empire" is about Jerry Casey, a graduate student struggling to be a writer:

> His professors spoke blithely of Shakespeare's "minor plays," Shaw's "failed efforts," Dickens's "unsuccessful pieces." Stories that Casey, stretched out on a flat rock under the blank Montana sky, had thrilled to and wondered at and anguished over, were assigned grades like so many frosh comp papers. B + to Somerset Maugham and Jane Austen. B- to C.S. Lewis and *Timon of Athens*. His own half-finished stories, Casey figured, the stories sweated and bled and wept over in his $83-a-month hole above a barber shop, were about an H-. On a good day....
>
> Casey walked. He walked on village streets at noon, over snowy athletic fields before dawn, in night woods where one clumsy step could break his unwary neck. While he walked, he agonized. He agonized because he was not Tolstoy or Shakespeare or even Maugham. He agonized because he was honest enough to know that he never would be Tolstoy or Shakespeare or Maugham. He complimented himself on being "at least" that honest with himself and agonized that his self-compliments showed a lack of artistic passion. When he wasn't walking and agonizing, he wrote. It was all H-. When he wasn't writing, he read Tolstoy. It was a definite A.

Jerry Casey's stories are "half-finished" because he gets stuck in the middle. He writes the first half, reads it over, and is immediately discouraged because it's not as good as the professional stories he reads every day. Casey suffers from the Tolstoy Syndrome, which affects only intelligent and self-aware people—and that includes most people who want to write. Their standards are high (how many of us can be Tolstoy?). "Whenever I apply myself to writing," said French author Jules Renard, "literature comes between us."

If you get stuck because nothing you write measures up to your own high standards, you're hamstringing yourself. You will only get better if you practice your craft, but you don't practice your craft because you're not already better at it. Even if you see this vicious circle taking place, you may feel helpless to stop it.

One rather elegant solution to this conundrum comes from veteran writer Robert Sheckley, in his essay "On Working Method." He suggests telling yourself that you're not really writing a story but only a *simulation* of a story. A simulation has action and characters and tension just like a real story, but since it's not a real story, the words you use aren't crucial. You don't worry about it, you just write it, working "rapidly and with a certain lightness of touch, as one would do a watercolor rather than a painting." In writing a simulation, you aren't competing with Tolstoy, who wrote real stories. The pressure is gone.

What Sheckley found, of course, was that his simulations looked pretty much like first drafts of his regular stories. He could "only write as I write, not much better or worse." But convincing himself he wasn't *really* writing got him unstuck.

Is this technique merely a mind game, a self-sanctioned self-deception? Yes, of course. But, then, the problem exists only in your mind in the first place. If you can manipulate your attitude into reducing the internal pressure you put on yourself, maybe you can get unstuck and finish the story.

If not, perhaps one of the other techniques discussed later in this chapter will help.

FEAR OF SUCCESS: THE NEVER-ENDING STORY

Sometimes the problem isn't fear of failure but fear of success. *If I finish this story,* the anxiety goes, *I'll have to start another one. And I don't have another idea. And maybe that other story won't go as well as this one.* So you don't finish. Instead you spend your time polishing what's already there, or planning various endings, or rewriting the opening even though the forty-two people who have read the current opening all say it's terrific.

Sometimes the fear of success takes a different form. You finish the story, but you never mail it out. It's finished, but it could be *better.* So you take it to an endless series of workshops (that's where the forty-two people saw it) to avoid testing yourself in the marketplace.

If such fears keep you stuck, you need to give yourself artificial deadlines. Tell yourself, *I will mail this story by December 3* (or May 14, or August 8). Tell everyone else, too: fellow workshop participants, your spouse, your mother, your kids. Ask them to ask you whether the story's gone out. Make it such a big deal that you *must* finish polishing or you'll feel like the biggest fool in the world. Then send the thing out. While it's making the rounds, get a copy of *Rotten Rejections: A Literary Companion* (edited by Andre Bernard, Pushcart Press, 1990). This compilation of rejections received by other writers will reassure you that rejection can be not only survived but vanquished. How can you feel singled out for personal failure when Sherwood Anderson, Jane Austen, John Barth, Gustave Flaubert, Jean Auel, Tony Hillerman, Erle Stanley Gardner, and Pearl S. Buck were all rejected first? (Buck, upon submission of *The Good Earth,* the book later responsible for her Nobel

Prize in Literature, was told that "the American public is not interested in anything on China.")

Then—this is important—begin another story immediately. Forget about the one in the mail. The one that counts is the one you're writing right now.

LITERARY FOGGINESS: WHAT'S SUPPOSED TO HAPPEN NEXT?

Sometimes reluctance to work on a manuscript comes for a very good reason: You don't know what's supposed to happen next in the story. Either you started the work hoping inspiration would appear along the way and it hasn't, or you've written yourself into a corner. In this case, so-called writer's block is actually a positive thing (although it won't feel like it). Like fatigue in a convalescent, your block is signaling you that you're not yet ready to be doing so much. You need to stop (no problem if you've already stopped), go back to the beginning of the work, and take some time to plan.

The previous chapter discussed how to plan the middle of your book, and I won't repeat my advice here. The point is that if you find yourself reluctant to even think about your manuscript, it could be you're not thinking about it enough. Instead of forcing yourself to write the next scene, let the keyboard sit idle and invest thinking time in your characters and plot. Scribble notes, if you like. Do you understand what your characters want? Could they maybe want something else you've overlooked? What's at stake in their story? Can you raise the stakes? Has the plot come to a standstill? What are some other directions it might take—even seemingly wild directions? Does anything about these scribbled notes excite you? Does that excitement suggest something you might want to write?

When you hit on something interesting, write it, even if it wasn't the direction you'd originally envisioned. Your original vision was foggy anyway; this might be better. If it doesn't fit with the first part of the story, don't worry about it now. In the second draft you can revise the beginning to fit this new middle.

WRONG DIRECTION:
I LEFT MY HEART IN CHAPTER THREE

The above advice also applies to a different cause of getting stuck. In this version, you know where you're going. You've worked out the whole story or novel in your mind, or you've outlined it on paper, and when you started to write it you were very interested. Then something happened. You've stuck to your outline, but now you hate the idea of sitting down to write. Also, the characters are behaving oddly. They're overreacting emotionally to simple occurrences. They're saying or doing things that strike you as out of character, but that they must say for your plot to work. They're making long speeches explaining to other characters why they're doing what they're doing, because without those speeches the reader won't understand their actions.

All of these are symptoms of a wrong turn in the story. Characters who overreact indicate that the situation itself isn't interesting enough, so you're trying to rev up the excitement level with histrionics. Out-of-character actions indicate either that your plot is wrong for these people or these people are the wrong ones to be inhabiting your plot. Long "this is why I behaved like that" speeches indicate a gap in characterization. If we know these people well enough, their actions should make sense to us without lengthy explanation. It's only when you haven't shown what your people are really like that we need after-the-fact explanations of their behavior.

In each of these cases, the solution is the same. Abandon the outline. It doesn't work. You now have two choices. If your characters are taking off in directions you didn't anticipate, rejoice and go with them. This means that even if your plot is now dead, your characters are still very much alive. Follow their lead and see if a new plot emerges from the unplanned actions you now prefer to write.

But if abandoning the outline and giving your characters their heads doesn't get your creative juices flowing again, you'll have to try something more drastic. Read over the story or novel. Where was the last place you were genuinely interested? Was it the second scene? Chapter three? Wherever that point occurred, discard everything after it. Then sit down and build a new plot on what's left.

This takes courage; you might be discarding weeks or even months of work. But there's no point in keeping scenes that merely mire you more deeply in apathy toward your own fiction. If you aren't interested in it, why should anyone else be? Cut your losses, keep what you can, and treat the story as a brand-new project.

TECHNIQUES TO KEEP YOU WRITING

But how can you do any of these things—write a story "simulation," conclude nonproductive polishing, rethink your direction, or go back to your first wrong turn—if you can't even make yourself sit down at your desk and write? Not anything. At all.

Various writers have devised techniques to break their personal writer's block. Try whichever ones you think might work for you.

Gene Wolfe, author of the much-praised tetralogy *Book of the New Sun,* refuses to allow himself to consume any words until he starts writing again. No books, magazines, newspapers, TV, radio, or unnecessary conversation. Eventually he gets so bored with this verbal Sahara that he returns to his typewriter. The longest he's ever been able to hold out is four days.

Some morning writers set a minimum number of pages they must write every day before they allow themselves to take up the other parts of their lives. Depending on your other commitments, this might range from half a page to five or eight pages (for full-time prolific writers).

Science-fiction writer Frederik Pohl, who turns out four pages a day, seven days a week, reports that sometimes his stint takes forty-five minutes, sometimes eighteen hours. But it gets done.

(It should be noted that this doesn't mean Pohl produces a novel every one hundred days [400 pages divided by 4 pages per day]. He's prolific, but not that prolific. Many of the pages will be revised or discarded.)

Other writers frame their commitment to writing in time, not page count. Flannery O'Connor wrote that she would sit at her desk from 9:00 A.M. to noon every day. During that time no writing might get done, but nothing else was allowed to get done, either. And if an idea did present itself, she said, "I am there ready for it."

Many writers use "triggers" to get themselves primed to write when the pump has gone dry. Reading good fiction triggers in some a desire to write their own stories. For Valerie Sherwood, author *of Lisbon,* the opposite was true: She reports that for years she triggered herself with a "ludicrously awful" novel, so badly written that it instantly inspired confidence that she could write a better one. Other authors use specific music to undam the creative flow. Still others keep two projects going at all times and, when one goes stale, switch to the other until their unconscious solves whatever narrative problem was blocking progress on the first piece.

There are writers who rely on physical activity. John Kessel, author of *Good News From Outer Space,* jogged on the same days he wrote.

> The fact that I could make myself run three days a week, week-in, week-out, good weather or bad, summer or winter, was a great help to me in writing the book. If I had the willpower for one, I had the willpower for the other. Also, running is a good opportunity to daydream about your story, characters, plot. Many times solutions came to me while I was jogging.

Some writers even welcome blocks. Jack Dann, author of *The Man Who Melted*, treats such "slow periods" as the way his unconscious lets him know it wants more material. He uses the time to research, read "anything that interests me," and he trusts his creative mind to ferment until it's ready to again decant.

Finally, some writers use rewards to entice themselves through difficult writing times. Finish three pages and you can have a beer. Finish the story and you can go see the movie you want. If you're disciplined enough not to cheat on your own reward system, this too can get you unstuck.

TECHNIQUES THAT WON'T GET YOU UNSTUCK

Richard McKenna, author of the best-selling novel *The Sand Pebbles* and the equally wonderful essay on creativity "Journey With a Little Man," relates in that essay his discouragement midway through writing the novel. For a time, he says, he became convinced that the answer to getting unstuck was to divorce his wife and move to the desert, where he could write uninterrupted by the demands of domesticity. Eventually he came to his senses. He kept both his wife and his geographical location—North Carolina—and finished the novel anyway.

Unless your external circumstances are very unusual, changing them won't cure writer's block. The way to get unstuck is not to shed your spouse, career, national citizenship, or material possessions. Quitting your job will give you more time to write, but it won't make you write more, or better. Moving to Paris can be interesting, but it won't turn you into Hemingway. Whatever mires you in the middle of your story comes from inside, not outside, and that's where you'll have to deal with it.

NOVELS: SETTLING IN FOR THE LONG HAUL

Sometimes you get stuck not because of the content of your story, but because of its size. A novel can seem an overwhelming undertaking: three hundred pages (or more—sometimes much more). How will you sustain your vision that long? How will you keep yourself going? How long does writing a novel take, anyway?

Since these questions are most likely to strike somewhere in the middle of your book, this chapter seems an appropriate place to answer them. Seen from the middle, a novel can seem an endless task. But there are ways to make it more manageable.

The basic principle is to break everything down into smaller pieces: chapters, time, page count. Specifically:

- Don't tell yourself, *Now I'm sitting down to write a novel.* Tell yourself, *Now I'm sitting down to start the scene where Martha sneaks onto a Greyhound for Memphis.* Concentrate on just that scene, giving it everything you've got; one scene isn't that overwhelming. And by putting the rest of the task out of your mind while you write, you won't fall into the trap of doing a hasty job because "there's so much else to cover" or because you're "saving some of the good stuff for later." There is no later. Write your best now.

- Track something. Keep records of the number of pages you write every week, or the percentage of chapters completed, or points of view used in various scenes. Tape this growing record on the wall over your desk. If you have a taste for this sort of thing, make a chart (I know one writer who actually graphs his output on an X-Bar control chart). You can also print out completed pages daily, or weekly, or as you finish an electronic file. The point is to have something tangible that grows over time, concrete evidence of progress.

- Create deadlines for yourself. These must be kept at least a little flexible, so you don't strangle those lovely unforeseen possibilities as you write. Even so, saying, "I'm working on chapter five" doesn't have the same purposeful effect as saying, "I'm going to finish chapter five in the next two weeks, and the whole first part by Memorial Day." This helps prevent any self-indulgent dawdling. Nor do deadlines mean you compromise quality. Charles Dickens wrote his greatest novels on deadline for serial publication. Anthony Trollope, who must have been disciplined to a frightening degree, set his watch on the desk while he wrote, and produced one page every fifteen minutes. If he varied from this, he either wrote faster or slowed down. After twelve pages he stopped for the day.

  You don't have to do that (would you *want* to?), but you might find that some looser, individually set deadlines make a novel seem more manageable.

How long should the whole process take? There's no consensus whatsoever on this. Annie Dillard, Pulitzer-prize-winning author of *The Writing Life,* says authoritatively that it takes between two and ten years to write a good book—but where does that leave Joyce Carol Oates, who appears to produce a novel every fifteen minutes? Or William Faulkner, who wrote *As I Lay Dying* in six weeks? Or John Steinbeck, who finished *The Grapes of Wrath* in five months? On the other hand, Joseph Heller went nineteen years between *Catch 22* and *Something Happened.*

The truth is, writing a novel takes as long as it takes. You may be a fast writer, or one who, like Joseph Conrad, works much more slowly ("In the course of that working day of eight hours I write three sentences, which I erase before leaving the table in despair."). You may have other commitments that severely limit your writing time, or you may be able to spend several hours every day at the keyboard. You may have a clear idea of your novel before you begin (those books go faster), or you may have to spend time and pages discovering what you want to say. There are so many variables that to measure yourself against another writer's timetable isn't useful.

What is useful is devising some system—self-imposed deadlines, writing appointments, schedules—to keep at the novel steadily. If five weeks go by without producing a paragraph, followed by a week in which you write fifteen thousand words, you *will* eventually get the book written. But it will be harder to recapture the tone after such a long fallow period, and it will be harder to trust your ability to repeat the marathon at will. Try to build up a habit of steady writing that you can trust to hold over time.

And, eventually, a day will come when you look up and realize you're more than three-quarters of the way through the book. You did it. You're past the middle. All the clichés suddenly seem true: You can see the light at the end of the tunnel, the path out of the woods, the calm after the storm.

You're approaching the ending.

STILL MORE EXERCISES FOR MIDDLES

1. If you're stuck in the middle of a piece of fiction, try to determine why. Fear of failure? Fear of success? Literary fogginess? Wrong direction? Once you've determined the cause, pick a solution from the appropriate section of this chapter and try it. *(Really try it.)* If you don't know why you're stuck, pick a solution from the section "Techniques to Keep You Writing."

2. If you're habitually stuck, repeat the first exercise following chapter three. Did it help?

3. If you're still stuck, read a biography of a writer who found writing torturous: Joseph Conrad, Jessamyn West, Dorothy Parker.

Did this erode your block by showing you that you're in very good company?

4. If you're not stuck in your current piece of fiction, try outlining the rest of the story before you write it. After the story is done, evaluate the usefulness of the outline. Did it increase your confidence, aid the story's clarity, or generate new incidents? Or not?

PART THREE

Endings
·················

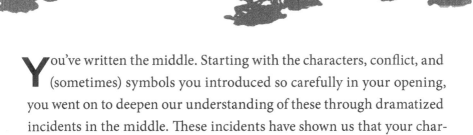

CHAPTER 7
SATISFYING ENDINGS: DELIVERING ON THE PROMISE

You've written the middle. Starting with the characters, conflict, and (sometimes) symbols you introduced so carefully in your opening, you went on to deepen our understanding of these through dramatized incidents in the middle. These incidents have shown us that your character is capable of change. The same incidents have made vivid the forces that will collide at your climax.

We can just *feel* these forces gathering. People are on the verge of being pushed into action, or disasters are on the edge of occurring, or secrets are about to be disclosed, or a deadline is almost here, or a situation has become so intolerable that it's obvious *somebody* is about to bring it toppling down around everybody else's ears. Whatever the specific events of your story, your middle has made it clear that things can't go on this way much longer. Something has to give.

Then a peaceful compromise is found and the story is over.

Huh?

Well, why not? Aren't compromises sometimes found in real life? Isn't everyone in favor of peaceful negotiation? And isn't it true that often people just have to live with bad situations indefinitely? Why can't a story end that way?

Because your story showed us forces in opposition to each other. Forces we expected to see collide in some way: quietly in a quiet story, noisily in a more dramatic one. But a collision of some sort we surely must have. You *promised*.

This is the clearest explanation of why some story endings work and others do not. At its beginning, a story makes the kind of implicit promise we've discussed throughout this book. In the middle, the development of both characters and conflict extends that promise by arranging forces in opposition to each other. We see, through skillfully chosen patterns of events, various problems and tensions come closer and closer to collision. Then comes the ending. It must use those same characters, conflicts, problems, and tensions to *show* us the collision (the climax).

If the ending tries to use different characters (such as the cavalry riding over the hill at the last minute), the story will fail. If the ending tries to switch to some other last-minute conflict, the story will fail. If the ending tries to evade the promised collision (by, for instance, a peaceful compromise in which no one loses anything), the story will fail. You cannot, in other words, promise apples and deliver oranges. The middle of your story—how you've developed the implicit promise—determines your ending.

This isn't to say that there is only one possible ending for any story. There may be more than one. But the ending chosen must complete what has been promised, not violate it.

Let's look again at that "favorite because it's so well known" example, *Gone With the Wind*. The forces lined up here are Scarlett's obsession with Ashley, Rhett's love for Scarlett, Ashley's inability to either leave Melanie or kiss off Scarlett, the pressures exerted on the aristocratic South by the Civil War, and Scarlett's single-minded pursuit of money and security, even at the expense of "ladylike" behavior. At the ending, of course, these forces result in Scarlett's losing Rhett and the South's losing the war. The outcome of the Civil War was beyond Margaret Mitchell's novelistic control, but the ending she chose for her characters was not the only one possible.

The book might, for instance, have ended with Scarlett and Rhett together, *if* Mitchell had portrayed Scarlett as changing significantly as a result of intense experiences (Alexandra Ripley certainly thought this possible; she did it in the sequel, *Scarlett)*. What *Gone With the Wind* promises is neither a happy nor an unhappy ending to its central romance, but rather a tumultuous story faithful to the larger history of the aristocratic South *as it perceived itself.* This, it delivered. Had Mitchell made the ending one with a sudden enlightened acceptance of the perceptions of some other group—abolitionists or freed slaves or crackers or Yankees, or contemporary civil rights groups—she would have ruined her novel. She wouldn't have played fair with the implicit promise of the first three-quarters of the book.

How do you find an ending that delivers? First, think carefully about what your story has promised the reader, both emotionally and intellectually. Vicarious terror? Vicarious love? Justice? The answer to a problem? An insight into contemporary life? The feeling that life isn't so bad after all? A view of a workable alternate society? A warm and cozy feeling?

Second, think carefully about the forces you've set in conflict throughout your middle. What are they? Can you list them? Which ending would bring them into plausible, satisfying collision, leaving some victorious and others vanquished? Which ones have you made promises about from the beginning?

As usual, this complex set of questions is easiest to grasp through an example. Suppose you've used the middle of our ongoing domestic drama (Martha, Sam, Jane) to develop all the following elements: (1) Martha's feelings of worthlessness and her desire to escape her life; (2) Sam's inarticulate love for his daughter; (3) Sam's workaholic nature, which leaves him little time for anything but his job; (4) Sam's ability to change if the pressure is strong enough; (5) Jane's destructive jealousy of Martha; (6) the local police's crackdown on drugs as an election approaches; (7) Martha's best friend's attempts at suicide, due to depression. Now you're ready to write the ending. Which of these forces do you want to be victorious? Depending on what your beginning and middle promised the reader, here are some possible endings:

- You've made an implicit promise that the reader will gain some painful insights into life on the streets. At your ending, Martha, frightened by police raids and distraught by her friend's suicide, tries to escape her own pain and overdoses on heroin. Despite her parents' frantic concern, she dies. Sometimes, your novel says, love is just not enough to save someone.

- You've made an implicit promise that the reader will find confirmation of traditional values through people she wants to identify with. Sam, driven by fear for his daughter, chooses her welfare over an important business meeting in Tokyo. With the aid of a sympathetic narcotics officer, and over his selfish wife's protests, Sam takes to the mean streets to find Martha. A crucial lead comes from Martha's best friend, hospitalized after her suicide attempt. Sam finds Martha, gets her into a drug program, and slowly Martha reconnects with her father—but not with her mother, who leaves. Sam gets custody. Martha gets clean. Your reader gets an affirmation of the power of love.

- You've promised black comedy: irreverent, hip, darkly hilarious. Martha becomes the mistress of a Colombian drug lord. When he's killed, she takes over the operation, becomes fabulously rich, and hires Sam, an attorney, as her legal advisor. Jane thinks her daughter's wealth comes from producing action-adventure movies in Panama, and wants to act in one of them herself. After all, she played the lead in her high-school play thirty years ago. Martha must acquire a Spanish movie company, keep her operations out of court, and satisfy her mother's narcissistic jealousy or Jane could blow the whistle on them all. Martha succeeds at all this. Your novel says that nothing is sacred: not motherhood, not daughterhood, not law, not art. (If you think stories can't make comic promises about crime and death, read Jimmy Breslin's novel *The Gang That Couldn't Shoot Straight.* Or see the Emily Lloyd movie *Cookie.*)

Which of these novels would you rather read? Which would you rather write? Whatever your answer, the basic point is the same: The ending dramatizes the triumph of some of the forces developed in the middle, which in turn were set in motion by the characters and conflict introduced in the beginning.

That is *what* your ending must accomplish. *How* you accomplish it is by controlling the two parts common to most story endings: the climax and the denouement.

CLIMAXES THAT DO

The climax, then, can be defined as whatever big event the forces in your story have been building toward. If a character is going to change, this is the experience that finally demonstrates that change (although earlier experiences may also play a part). If a problem is going to get solved, this is where the protagonist solves it. This is where the villain makes his last big fight, the lovers are united, the family tension finally explodes, the quest reaches its goal (for good or ill), the decisive confrontation occurs. This is the scene the moviemakers are after when they option your novel. In a short story, this is the scene where readers discover why they've been reading the story. The payoff.

To succeed, a climax must do four things:

1. *The climax must satisfy the view of life implied in your story*—as discussed above.

2. *The climax must deliver emotion.* An emotionally neutral climax will disappoint readers. They should feel whatever your characters feel. If your characters don't feel anything in particular, this is not the climax.

3. *The climax must deliver an appropriate level of emotion.* This means that the level of drama in the climax must match the level of drama throughout the story. Too much drama will short-circuit a restrained, quiet story; too little drama will seem flat in a story already festooned with murder, betrayal, war, sex, car chases, or other strong action. Thus, if your story has focused on domestic irritation, ending it with a character's blowing his brains out won't work. It will feel contrived, as if you were trying to inject some artificial drama. Similarly a saga of violent gangland warfare shouldn't end with a quiet talk between the leaders and a subtle symbol of ambiguous hope. In context, that will feel flat.

4. *The climax must be logical to your plot and your story.* As we've already seen, the climactic scene must grow naturally out of the actions that preceded it, which in turn must have grown naturally out of the personalities of the characters. The term *deus ex machina* ("god from the machine") describes those plots in which the climax depends on the arrival of some new, outside force: Zeus, the cavalry, a random bus accident, instant enlightenment. *Deus ex machina* is not a compliment. Nor should your climax turn on a coincidence; this was acceptable (barely) when Dickens did it in the nineteenth cen-

tury, but no longer (except in some types of comedy). Make sure your climax is not only plausible for your characters, but pretty close to inevitable.

I say "pretty close" because it's still possible to surprise readers with an unexpected ending without violating the above criteria. Consider Tom Wolfe's novel *Bonfire of the Vanities*. The reader anticipates only two possible endings: The jury finds Sherman McCoy either guilty or not guilty. Instead, Wolfe surprises with a third outcome: a hung jury that means McCoy must go through the whole chaotic, exhausting, expensive, exploitive process again. The ending delivers on the novel's basic promise—a satiric look at a city that no longer works—while still catching us off guard.

THE RIGHT ENDING: A LITMUS TEST

A successful ending must be tied not only to the author's implicit promise and the forces dramatized in the middle, but also to the protagonist's nature. A test for your ending is this question: *If my protagonist were a radically different person, would this story still end the same way?* The answer should be *No*. If it's *Yes*—if the events of your book would be unaltered no matter *whom* they happened to—your ending will not feel convincing.

Consider one version of the ever-useful Sam. You've spent 350 pages establishing Sam as a man who neglects his family because he's afraid of emotional intimacy. He is, however, capable of change if a situation reaches crisis proportions. Jane is critical and unloving (which is part of the reason Sam avoids intimacy). Martha gets into increasing trouble until she finally disappears for four months. Your plot involves Sam's increasingly committed search for his daughter, his discovery that Jane supplied Martha with her first drugs, and Martha's desperate struggles to survive in a sleazy world she's not experienced enough to handle. What ending do you choose?

Let's say Sam succeeds in finding Martha. He persuades her to come home. Out of desperation, she agrees, and Sam resolves to do better as a father this time around. Jane asks for a divorce; she can see that while Sam's new fumbles at intimacy may be admirable, they're not going to include her, and she can't bear to once more be kept at arm's length.

Would this ending work if Sam were a different person: sensitive, loving, devoted to family? No, because such a man wouldn't need to change. Would this ending work if Jane were a warm, dedicated doctor working hard to establish a methadone program in the inner city? No, because such a mother wouldn't have given Martha drugs in the first place, and such a compassionate version of Jane would probably have a much less destructive attitude toward her daughter. Would this ending work if Jane were a caring, although short-tempered, wife and mother? No, because she wouldn't leave Sam because of his emotional growth; she'd probably welcome it, although maybe fearfully. Would this ending work if Martha were a stronger, less confused child? No, because she either wouldn't have run away or else wouldn't agree to come back.

The ending wouldn't work with different personalities in the key roles. That's a good sign: Your ending grows naturally out of who your characters are. It's easy to see this about Sam, Jane, and Martha because this hypothetical novel is *about* relationships. But the principle holds true even when your story is more concerned with external events. *Bonfire of the Vanities* is mainly concerned with the breakdown of New York City. But the ending wouldn't work if Sherman McCoy were a nice guy (which he's not). First, he wouldn't agree to wear a wire in order to throw blame on his mistress, and second, we would be rooting too strongly for his exoneration. Wolfe's ending passes the character test.

Finding the right ending sometimes takes time. Once it took me thirteen years. In 1977 I tried to write a science-fiction story about people who never sleep. Every editor who rejected the story (they were legion) commented that the characters were interesting but the ending "felt unresolved." After three years of steady rejection, I put the story away.

Two years later, I tried to revise it. I still couldn't find a good ending. I didn't, at that point in my writing career, even know how to think about what made a good ending. It either "came" or it didn't. In this case, it didn't.

Eight years later, still interested in the idea, I again pulled the manuscript from my files. Now I could see why the ending failed. The conflict centered on antagonism between Sleepers and Sleepless in the same family. At the end, one of the Sleepless simply abandoned her antagonism. Nothing in the middle of the story prepared the reader for this change of heart—in fact, she was represented as a pretty relentless person. Yet there she was, abandoning her distrust of Sleepers for no other reason than *I* wanted her to.

I completely rewrote the story, now called "Beggars In Spain." This time I concentrated on the middle. I dramatized the Sleepless woman's political beliefs and her complicated relationships with various Sleepers. I showed situations in which she loved Sleepers, and situations in which she had real cause to distrust and hate them. When the climax comes, and the protagonist chooses to believe in a common humanity that transcends genetic differences, her choice is plausible. It has grown out of her personality, her experiences, and her perceptions. In other words, the choice fits with the protagonist's character, not the author's plot needs.

This time the story sold immediately, eventually winning an award. The ending worked because it had grown out of the character's deepest self.

A FINAL WORD ON THE CLIMACTIC SCENE

The climax must be in proportion to the length of your story.

In novels, the climax usually occupies at least a chapter; it may take several chapters. In a short story, the length of the climactic scene depends on what kind of story you're writing (more on this in the next chapter), but in general it, too, should not be rushed. If you have twenty pages setting up a tense situation, the resolution should not flash by in two brief paragraphs. It won't feel important enough.

How long is long enough? There's no one answer to that; it depends on the specific work. Consider your story as a jewelry setting, and your climax the diamond. The diamond may not be as large as the gold around it, but it should be large enough so it doesn't seem insignificant by comparison.

THE DENOUEMENT: "MARRYIN' AND BURYIN'"

Everything after the climax is called the *denouement*, whose function is to wrap up the story. Mark Twain referred to the denouement as "the marryin' and the buryin'." It shows us two things: the consequences of the plot and the fate of any characters not accounted for in the climax.

Consider again Michael Crichton's best-selling novel *Jurassic Park*. The climactic scene, which consists of several chapters, concerns the cloned dinosaurs' attacks on the human compound and the humans' counterattack with government firepower, which destroys the entire island. After the climax, however, Crichton is still left with a few dinosaurs that escaped to the mainland even before chapter one. He's also left with some survivors of the catastrophe on the island; presumably readers will want to know what happened to these people. Crichton's two-and-a-half-page denouement satisfies readers' questions about both people and reptiles.

In a short story there may or may not be a denouement. In some stories—especially those that are very short—the climactic moment, in which the protagonist undergoes a change, may also be the last moment of the story. What happens to her after that is left to the reader's imagination. In other stories, the denouement may consist of a sentence, a paragraph, or a brief scene clarifying what happens to the character after she changes.

For instance, consider Bill Barich's story "Hard to Be Good," which chronicles the summer Shane is sixteen. At the start of the summer (and the story), Shane acts so irresponsibly, using drugs and running afoul of the law, that his frustrated grandparents ship him off to his mother and her third husband. At the story's climax, after an eventful summer, Shane helps his friend Grady and his stepfather Bentley burn marijuana plants growing in Bentley's backyard. Shane is afraid their presence might cause further legal complications for his family. He has learned to think in terms of both consequences and other people.

The story could easily have ended there. But Barich adds a single paragraph of denouement to let us know that at summer's end Shane returns to his grandparents, while planning to visit his mother and stepfather again next summer. This denouement satisfies our curiosity about Shane's future and about his grandparents, who were sympathetically presented. Similarly, if *your* story leaves questions unanswered or characters dangling, you might consider adding a denouement to satisfy reader curiosity.

A successful denouement has three characteristics: closure, brevity, and dramatization.

Closure means you give your readers enough information about the fate of the characters for them to feel that the book really is over. Obviously, you don't have to describe the rest of the protagonist's life; you don't even have to really tell whether he achieves his goal. Both the waitress in Raymond Carver's "Fat" and the Scarlett of *Gone With the Wind* are still unsatisfied. But Carver and Mitchell tell us enough so that we know what they'll do about it: The waitress will change her life, and Scarlett will plot to get Rhett back. Similarly, the adult survivors of *Jurassic Park* are being detained indefinitely by the Costa Rican government and the escaped dinosaurs are still loose, but the denouement tells us enough for us to grasp their situation and to see that the whole problem is going to repeat itself. You, too, must show just enough of your characters' futures so that your reader doesn't feel like he's left hanging.

Sometimes a new writer will say—especially about a short story—"Well, I didn't *want* to tell what happened to the characters. I wanted to leave the book ambiguous and open-ended. I want readers to decide for themselves what happened." This is usually a response to criticism that the story feels as if it "just stopped."

Unfortunately, the "let readers decide for themselves" stance is usually a failed defense. Readers don't want to decide what happened to the characters. They want *you* to decide, on the dual grounds that you're the writer and that they've just read four hundred pages of your prose anticipating this very information you're now withholding. Except in a few rare instances, a story is not helped by being left, from the readers' point of view, uncompleted. Provide the closure your readers want. Write the denouement.

When you do, keep it brief. *Brevity* is important to a denouement because if it goes on too long, it will leach all emotion from the climax. End while your reader is still affected by your big scene. Anything else will feel anticlimactic.

As a rule of thumb, the more subtle and low-key the climax in action and tone, the briefer the denouement should be. The climax of *Jurassic Park* is highly dramatic: the destruction of an entire island. Such intense action creates enough momentum to carry the reader through the two-and-a-half-page denouement without risking anticlimax. At the other end of the intensity spectrum is a quiet short story in which the climactic action is a change of perception inside the protagonist's head. If such a story has a denouement at all, it will probably be only a sentence or two.

Similarly, *dramatization* ensures that your denouement feels like part of the story, not a chunk of exposition tacked on after the story's over. Try to show what happens to your characters by showing them in action. *Jurassic Park* ends with a conversation between one of the survivors and a researcher not connected with the dinosaur disaster. *Gone With the Wind's* denouement portrays Scarlett alone, but she's having an intense conversation with herself. A note of caution, however: Whatever action you choose to dramatize, your denouement should be fairly mild. Otherwise it may compete with the climax.

TO EPILOGUE OR NOT TO EPILOGUE

The *Jurassic Park* denouement is set off in its own chapter, which is called "Epilogue: San Jose." What do you gain by labeling your denouement an epilogue?

Although there are exceptions, contemporary novelists generally set the denouement apart in an epilogue only if it differs significantly from the main narrative in time or place, or if it's going to be in a radically different style.

Thus, the action *of Jurassic Park's* epilogue occurs off the island, in a city more than twenty miles away, days after the destruction of the island dinosaurs. The epilogue in *Bonfire of the Vanities* takes place a year after the main story and consists entirely of a newspaper article in the *New York Times*. The epilogue of Margaret Atwood's *The Handmaid's Tale* occurs hundreds of years after the book's action. The protagonist is dead. This epilogue takes the form of a symposium transcript: historians discussing the novel events from their own far-future, radically different perspective.

If the events of your novel require wrapping up in a different place, time, or narrative style, consider calling the wrap-up an epilogue. This alerts the reader that something different is coming up, softening the sense of discontinuity from the main narrative. The label *epilogue* can also shift reader expectations about tone, from the immediacy of the climax to a longer, more contemplative view of what that climax might mean. " 'An epilogue,' " wrote John Irving's character T.S. Garp," 'is more than a body count. An epilogue, in the disguise of wrapping up the past, is really a way of warning us about the future.' " (Irving evidently believed Garp; the epilogue in *The World According to Garp* warns us about the futures of fourteen characters.)

THE SPECIAL CASE OF THE SERIES BOOK

Every book in a series (except the last—and are you *sure* you're not going to write another one?) bears a special burden. In addition to standing on its own as a satisfying reading experience, it must also leave the door open for the next book. This means that things can't be too thoroughly wrapped up. If the hero is dead, the town destroyed, the war over, and the lovers married, what will you write about?

Actually there are three kinds of series books, and what you write about depends on which kind you're creating. A series like Sue Grafton's "alphabet mysteries" (*A Is For Alibi,* etc.) features the same protagonist in every book. This means detective Kinsey Millhone must finish every book alive, still willing to be a detective, and enough unchanged that readers who enjoyed her in one book won't find her with a different personality in the next book. If you write this kind of series, you need to make sure your protagonist ends up in roughly the same professional and emotional place she started. You'll have to emphasize plot over character development.

In the second type of series, you have more freedom because the books don't feature the same character but only the same setting, or the same family, or maybe just the same universe. Two very different examples: John Jakes's *Kent Chronicles,* which follow several generations of an American family; and Isaac Asimov's science-fiction *Foundation* series. In both series, the protagonist of one book doesn't necessarily appear in the next. Only the conceptual framework—a chain of descendants or a future controlled by the predictive genius of "psychohistory"—remains the same. Within that framework, anything can happen. Characters can change, die, or exit the story. When the author finishes one story within the framework, he shifts focus to another protagonist.

The third kind of series also permits characters to change, but without shifting focus from the initial protagonists. These books, usually *literary* rather than formulaic, don't allow readers to expect that the protagonist will return to essentially unchanged circumstances in the next installment. Both circumstances and protagonist evolve. John Updike's novels about Harry "Rabbit" Angstrom, which follow Rabbit throughout four decades of American middle-class life, are a good example of this kind of series. The Rabbit of the fourth book, *Rabbit At Rest,* is not the same scared, irresponsible, blindly groping boy of the series' opener, *Rabbit, Run*—although he's still Rabbit. Similarly Updike's series of short stories about Joan and Richard Maple, written over twenty years, gives us a couple who know considerably more about each other at their eventual divorce than they knew as newlyweds.

So the first thing you need to know is which kind of series you're writing, since this controls how much your protagonists and their circumstances may change.

If it's the first type of series, you simply invent a new problem for your permanent protagonist.

If it's the second type, leave something in the plot situation unresolved, to be taken up in later book(s) by different characters. In Asimov's series, for instance, the predictions left by psychohistorian Hari Seldon aren't exhausted by the end of the first story (in fact, they've hardly begun).

If you're writing the third type of series, prepare for the next book by leaving your characters some unsettled personal issues—what psychologists call "unfinished business." If your characters are realistic human beings, there will always be unsettled issues, because as the characters age they react to new circumstances with old psychological equipment. Updike's Richard Maple, for instance, is unable or unwilling to confine his sexual interest to his wife, and from this comes the first betrayal, sending resentments and complexities throughout twenty years of marriage.

The main point here is that in both the first and second types of series, you don't wait until the end of the book to set up the next book. If the plot situation will be left unresolved enough to spawn many stories with many characters, it has to be large scaled and complex. If the characters will be able to support additional stories about them, they too will have to be multilayered and complex. The place to create complexity is not the end of the book, but the middle—as we discussed in chapters three and four. That's where characterization is deepened, situations complicated. That's where you leave doors open for future volumes.

Series capability is a function of good middles. That's not surprising; throughout this book we've seen that all good endings grow out of what happens in the middle. Series novels merely extend that planning into subsequent volumes.

CHECKLIST FOR SUCCESSFUL ENDINGS

Check your proposed ending against the following list:

- Does the climax grow logically out of the specific experiences that this character had in the middle of the story?

- Have the events of the middle of the story prepared the reader for the change in character change (if there is one) or is it a "come to suddenly realize" change?

- Are all the various forces present at the climax also present in the middle of the story—no *deus ex machina* late arrivals?

- Is the fate of each secondary character in the climax or the denouement consistent with how these people were portrayed in the middle?

- Does the ending deliver on the promise implicit in the middle of the story—that is, does it fulfill reader expectations you developed by the events, tone, and worldview of the middle?

- Is your climax in proportion to the middle of the story— neither too different from it in level of drama nor too short in terms of total page count?

If the answer to all of these questions is *yes*, you've got a viable ending— *and* a good middle.

Dante would be pleased.

EXERCISES FOR ENDINGS

1. Choose a story, at least twenty pages long, that you've never read before. Read four pages, put the story down, and list all the expectations you've already formed about the story. Include anything that occurs to you: style, characters, situation, conflict, outcome, worldview. Now finish the story. Were your expectations met? Did the genre the story belongs to contribute to your expectations being met?

2. Identify the climax of the story you've just read. Where does it start? End? What forces, stated or implied, come together to form the climax? How had each been developed earlier in the story?

3. Look at the denouement of the same story, if it has one. How does it wrap up the plot? Does it account for all major characters (in a short story, there may be only one major character)? What would be lost if the denouement were omitted?

4. Find a reader whose opinion you trust. Ask her all the above questions about one of *your* finished stories. Did you learn anything about how your story appears to a reader?

5. Try plotting a different ending for a short story—your own or someone else's—that you like very much. What character changes earlier in the story would be necessary for this new ending to work?

CHAPTER 8

THE VERY END: LAST SCENE, LAST PARAGRAPH, LAST SENTENCE

Much of what was said in the last chapter about endings applies to both novels and short stories. Both need endings that fulfill the promise of the story, grow out of character, come to an emotional climax, and are well prepared for by a strong middle. But novels and short stories differ sharply in one respect: the emphasis placed on the very end.

The truth is that although everything in any work of fiction should contribute to the whole, the last few paragraphs of a novel are relatively unimportant. A novel is so long that by the time the reader comes to the end, 99 percent of the plot, character development, theme, and everything else are over. And since the structure of a novel usually requires a climax followed by a denouement, the very end of a novel is a time of decreasing tension. Nothing startling, new, or highly emotional is likely to turn up this late in such a lengthy tale.

A short story is much different. The climax may *be* the ending, as we saw in previous chapters. Even when an additional scene follows the climax, it is likely to carry heavy symbolic significance. And the shorter the story, the more important the last few paragraphs become.

In a certain kind of short story, the last sentence is especially crucial. To understand why, we need first to understand the distinction between two kinds of short stories—a distinction that applies much more to endings than to beginnings or middles.

RESOLUTION VERSUS RESONANCE

Short stories divide into two broad, overlapping categories: the traditional plotted story and what, for lack of a better name, we'll call the contemporary literary short story.

The traditional plotted story is easy to recognize. Its ending is like that of a novel: The plot complications are resolved, for better or worse, and the fates of all the major characters are made clear. This is the kind of story we all grew up on: "Cinderella" and "Peter Rabbit" and the mystery stories in *Boy's Life*. Cinderella lives happily ever after; Peter Rabbit is punished while Flopsy, Mopsy, and Cottontail get blueberries and cream; the youthful detectives solve the mystery. When the story's over, there are no loose ends.

A good example of an adult traditional plotted story is Shirley Jackson's much-anthologized "The Lottery." At the start of the story we see a New England town preparing for some sort of lottery. In the middle, the workings of the lottery are dramatized as the candidates are narrowed down to one "winner." In the concluding paragraphs the situation is clearly resolved: We learn what the lottery has been about, what happens to the winner, what is the role of the rest of the townspeople, and why we shouldn't hang around small New England towns in the spring.

Other well-known examples of the traditional plotted story are Charles Dickens's "A Christmas Carol," William Faulkner's "A Rose for Emily," and Arthur Conan Doyle's stories about Sherlock Holmes.

The ending of the contemporary literary short story, in contrast, may not seem to resolve anything, or to account for what happens to the characters. Indeed people who don't like this type of writing often finish a contemporary literary short story and say, "But nothing happened." Or "There isn't any ending— the story just stopped." Or even, "Am I missing the last page?" But the nonresolution of sit-

uation and plot is actually deliberate. Stories of this type aim at examining a situation but not resolving it *because* the situation itself is
ambiguous, interesting in and of itself without resolution, or impossible to resolve.

This is easiest to see in an example. Ernest Hemingway's well-known
story "A Clean, Well-Lighted Place" takes place in a Paris café, near closing time in the small hours of the morning. The protagonist, a middle-
aged waiter, observes several small events: the reluctance of an old man
to leave the well-lighted café and go home; the eagerness of a young waiter to leave work and go home to his wife; the glint of light on the metal
insignia of a soldier's uniform. After the café finally closes, the waiter
goes to another bar and has a drink, reciting to himself a version of the
Lord's Prayer in which "nada" has been substituted for most key words.
The story ends.

Obviously what happens to the waiter the rest of his life— or even the
rest of the night—is not important here. In that sense, the ending has no
resolution. What is important to Hemingway is making the reader *feel*
a situation in which life and death, youth and age, are evoked in various
ways through the symbols of light and darkness. The story doesn't resolve because not even Hemingway could neatly wrap up the question of
ever-approaching death. But the story *resonates:* It sets off in the reader
a complex intellectual and emotional reaction to the skillful rendering
of a meaningful situation. That is the whole point of the contemporary
literary short story. "Literature," writes critic Roland Barthes, "is the
question minus the answer."

In making this rough distinction, I don't mean to imply that traditional plotted stories don't raise questions or resonate in the mind. Good
ones certainly do. Nor do I mean to imply that contemporary literary
short stories are just a bunch of symbols stuck together, without a real
ending. Good ones have endings as well crafted as any traditional plotted

story. But it's a different kind of ending, dependent more on symbol and nuance than on resolution.

What makes an ending resonate? There's no simple answer. What resonates for one reader may be uninteresting, boring, or baffling to another. That's because the whole idea of "resonance" is that the ending strikes chords of recognition and meaning in the reader: *I, too, have felt that* or *I've always thought that but I never had words for it before* or just *I've wondered about that, too—it really happens, then.* For this resonance to work, you need a sensitive reader: one capable of making subtle connections between the world of the story and the world he lives in. Not all readers can—or want—to do that. A great many prefer to escape from this world into one that is more brightly colored, more exciting, or faster paced—without being reminded of the world they left behind. That's why contemporary literary short stories have a much smaller readership than do commercial novels.

From a writer's perspective, you create a resonant ending by suggesting connections between your story and a larger context, often through the use of symbols. The protagonist's action at the climax must mean *more* than it appears to. There are no easy prescriptions for doing this—we're talking about art here—but there *are* examples to study. Two are examined later in this chapter: Hemingway's "A Clean, Well-Lighted Place," mentioned earlier, and Stephen Minot's "Sausage and Beer." Both use common occurrences (respectively, prayer and coldness) as symbols to encompass more than what occurs in their stories—in other words, to make their stories *resonate* rather than *resolve.*

Do you want to write that kind of story? That's up to you. The point here is that by the time you reach the ending, you must know what kind of story you are writing. A traditional plotted story signals from the beginning that it *is* plotted. There is a clearly delineated problem, a plot is unfolding, characters are engaged in purposeful action or reaction. Readers easily pick up on these signals. They then expect a traditional resolution— that's part of the promise your story made—and will feel seriously cheated if they don't get it.

A contemporary literary short story also sends out signals. The beginning and middle may feature more ambiguous action. There is usually more use of symbol, more attention paid to nuances of language, less obvious plot. Such a story doesn't *have* to end up unresolved—some end more or less traditionally after all—but it *can* be left unresolved without violating the promise made to the reader.

Another clue is where a reader finds the story. In the so-called "little magazines"—periodicals that often pay only in copies—a knowledgeable reader will expect a preponderance of contemporary literary short stories. In mass-market magazines with huge circulations—*Ladies' Home Journal, Ellery Queen's Mystery Magazine, Playboy*—most of the stories will be traditional plotted fiction. Reader expectations adjust accordingly.

What does this mean for you, the writer? Another version of what we've said all along: Your ending must satisfy the expectations your story has raised. After you know which kind of ending you're writing, you can devise successful closing paragraphs.

THE ENDING OF A TRADITIONAL PLOTTED STORY

It's similar to the ending of a novel, and the same requirements apply (see the last chapter). However, because a short story is briefer and contains fewer characters, the climax sometimes includes the denouement; that is, we find out during the climactic scene what happened to everybody who counts, and so the story ends.

At the end of any story, something must be different from the beginning. Something must have changed in a meaningful way. An important consideration in writing the ending to a traditional plotted story is that this change should be embodied in an action. It's not enough to show that a character realizes something she didn't know before; she must do something about it or at least must resolve to do something about it. Anything less doesn't provide enough closure for the traditional plotted story.

For example, upon waking from his mystical travels with the Ghosts of Christmas Past, Present, and Future, Ebeneezer Scrooge doesn't merely think, "Whew! From now on I'll be a better man!" Dickens shows us Scrooge's change in action. Scrooge pledges money to charity, makes merry with his nephew Fred, raises Bob Cratchit's salary. (In fact, the function of Cratchit and family is to be abused by Scrooge before his conversion and aided afterward. That's why they're in the story.)

Similarly, "Flowers For Algernon" ends with a specific request from Charlie Gordon concerning the mouse that underwent the same failed I.Q.-enhancing operation as he did. This action dramatizes Charlie's return to his former simplicity and sweetness: "Please if you get a chanse put some flowrs on Algernons grave in the bak yard."

When you choose an action to dramatize whatever has changed from the beginning of your story, consider one additional criterion. The end of a story often delivers a dose of emotion—a rise in the emotional temperature of the narrative. Charlie Gordon's final request is moving because the reader knows that Charlie will share Algernon's death. The end of "The Lottery" sharply increases the level of horror. And the final action of "A Christmas Carol," a blessing from Tiny Tim, could hardly be more sentimentally optimistic. Whatever emotion your story as a whole seeks to convey, try to choose a final action that will evoke it in the reader.

THE ENDING OF A CONTEMPORARY LITERARY SHORT STORY

Much of what was said above also applies to the contemporary literary short story—but not all of it. This kind of story also evokes some emotion at the end, although the emotion may be mixed and ambiguous. There also needs to be a change of some sort from the beginning of the story to the end, and that change should be embodied in an action. However, the action may be very slight, and, as mentioned earlier, the full import of the change may be carried mostly through symbol.

For instance, the waiter of Hemingway's "A Clean, Well-Lighted Place" doesn't do much at the end of the story. He simply goes home, just as he always does. The experiences he has in the story won't change his external life at all. The only indication that he's even *had* an experience is his recitation of a nihilistic version of the Lord's Prayer. His night's observations have evidently brought out in him (or in the author through him) the feeling that since life must end in death, it is ultimately meaningless. The story embodies this realization in the mangled prayer, which then becomes a symbol for everything else that has happened in the story. The symbols, not the external action, are what carry the story's meaning.

One more example: Stephen Minot's story "Sausage and Beer." In this story a boy and his father set out to visit the father's brother, Uncle Theodore, who is in a state mental hospital. On the way the boy entertains various melodramatic notions about this uncle he's never met. ("'My Uncle Theodore,' I rehearsed silently, 'he's the cop killer.'") But instead the visit shocks the boy with its banality, with the utterly ordinary "quiet sound of madness." At the end of the story, father and son stop at a speakeasy (this is the 1930s) for sausage and beer. Food is there, and cheerful noise, and the warmth of the bar after multiple images of freezing cold. "We ate and drank quietly," ends the story, "lost in a kind of communion." The boy has made a passage into an adult realization, and the final action takes on the symbolism of religious ritual. It's not a traditional plotted story because nothing about Uncle Theodore's illness has really been resolved. Not much, in fact, even *happened*, except symbolically. But that's enough. To show that it's enough, the story ends with a powerful symbol.

Often that symbol will have been introduced at the beginning of the story, in the first paragraph. The first two lines of "Sausage and Beer" are, "I kept quiet for most of the trip. It was too cold to talk." By the end, father and son are still quiet but it is the quiet of "communion" blessed by the waiter's "benedictory smile." And the cold, referred to again and again throughout the story, has been replaced by comforting warmth. The use of the same symbolism at beginning and end creates a circular pattern that helps make even an open-ended story feel "finished."

Again, you might not want to write this kind of story. But as a writer, you should know that it exists, what its ending must accomplish, and how it uses symbols to do so. Many writers who start their careers with traditional plotted stories eventually become intrigued by the literary story and end up writing some of both (I did). And, of course, traditional plotted stories may also incorporate symbols into their action-based endings.

In summary:

- The ending of the contemporary literary short story may or may not be identical with the climax.

- The story usually makes its point through symbol rather than resolving anything through action.

- The symbols evolve throughout the story, frequently turning up as early as the first paragraph.

THE VERY, VERY END:
THE LAST PARAGRAPH
. . . .

Why would I think it worth my while—or yours—to include in this book a section focusing on a single paragraph?

Because the last paragraph of a short story is the power position—and within that position, the last sentence is the most powerful of all. Often—not infallibly, but often—the last sentence or paragraph evokes the theme of the entire story. Final sentences don't do this like Aesop's fables, flat-footedly stating a moral: *Don't count your chickens before they hatch. Slow and steady wins the race.* Instead, effective final paragraphs use action, symbol, or a character's thoughts to seamlessly comment on the story's meaning while also bringing the plot to a close.

As always, it's easiest to see this through example. Here are the last paragraphs of stories we've discussed in this chapter. Note how each evokes the story's theme:

> I nodded. All three of us nodded. Then the waiter brought a tray with the order, and the fat man left us with a quick, benedictory smile. We ate and drank quietly, lost in a kind of communion.
>> —"Sausage and Beer," a story about the need for, and difficulty of, making genuine contact with other people.

> P.P.S. Please if you get a chanse put some flowrs on Algernons grave in the bak yard.
>> —"Flowers For Algernon," a story about the complex interplay of intelligence and happiness.

> "It isn't fair, it isn't right," Mrs. Hutchinson screamed, and then they were upon her.
>> —"The Lottery," a story about the good of the individual versus the perceived good of a whole town.

"No, thank you," said the waiter and went out. He disliked bars and bodegas. A clean, well-lighted café was a very different thing. Now, without thinking further, he would go home to his room. He would lie in the bed and finally, with daylight, he would go to sleep. After all, he said to himself, it is probably only insomnia. Many must have it.

— "A Clean, Well-Lighted Place," a story about the inevitable fear of inevitable death.

The last sentences of novels, too, tend to imply the theme of the entire work. This is true even though, as I said earlier, the very end of a novel is relatively unimportant compared to that of a short story. Yet novelists also polish that final paragraph until it does more than just bring the action to a satisfactory close. Consider the thematic implications of these last paragraphs, taken from four otherwise very different novels:

"None of us is going anywhere, Dr. Grant," Guitierrez said, smiling. And then he turned, and walked back toward the entrance of the hotel.

—*Jurassic Park,* a story about an ecological disaster that has not been successfully corrected and possibly never can be.

We sat for a long time in silence, and then talked again of Conway as I remembered him, boyish and gifted and full of charm, and of the War that had altered him, and of so many mysteries of time and age and of the mind, and of the little Manchu who had been "most old," and of the strange ultimate dream of the Blue Moon. "Do you think he will ever find it?" I asked.

—*Lost Horizon,* by James Hilton, a novel about one man's discovery and loss of Shangri-La, the secret valley in the Himalayas that represents humanity's deepest longings: peace, agelessness, and the satisfying of all desire.

Torn paper was flying in the air over the victorious marchers; and now and then a scrap drifted down and brushed the face of the last captain of the *Caine.*

> —*The Caine Mutiny,* by Herman Wouk, a novel about a World War II naval mutiny, in which the protagonist learns which values matter and which don't: a personal victory amid a mismanaged bureaucracy.

You get down on your knees and tear open the bag. The smell of warm dough envelops you. The first bite sticks in your throat and you almost gag. You will have to go slowly. You will have to learn everything all over again.

> —*Bright Lights, Big City,* by Jay McInerney, a novel about a young man who since the death of his mother has buried his grief under a riot of wild, destructive living.

Sometimes the ending paragraph of a novel, as in short stories, deliberately echoes the opening paragraph. In Dan Wakefield's hilarious novel of 1960s sexual mores, *Starting Over,* the first and last paragraphs are identical single sentences: "Potter was lucky; everyone told him so." The first paragraph congratulates Phil Potter on his divorce; the last, on his remarriage. By using the same wording for two opposite events, author Wakefield slyly points up that Potter has learned nothing, grown not at all from his experiences. He has only come full circle.

Jean Auel, too, in her best-selling *Clan of the Cave Bear,* ends as she begins, with a scene of a child terrified at being separated from its mother. Here the parallel scenes bring some feeling of closure to a novel that isn't actually over, since it's the first in a four-book series. This circular device—like any other—can seem mechanical if it's forced on a book that doesn't warrant it, but when it *does* fit your story, it can be effective.

Notice that none of these last paragraphs use stiff, abstract language to underline their novels' themes. They aren't obtrusive. Indeed the careless reader might not register the paragraph's thematic significance at all, except unconsciously. That's all right. A good novel or short story can always be read on two levels: that of plot and that of meaning. So should a good last paragraph.

REWRITING: LOOKING FOR A FEW GOOD SENTENCES

So how do you get that polished last scene, evocative last paragraph, perfect last sentence? Through revision. The great Russian masters knew the importance of revision. Tolstoy rewrote *Anna Karenina* seventeen times (in longhand!). Vladimir Nabokov wrote, "I have rewritten—often several times—every word I have ever written. My pencils outlast their erasers."

Rewriting your ending is just as important as rewriting your beginning, and repays the effort just as strongly. A good beginning gains your reader's initial interest; a good ending makes your story linger in his memory after he closes the book or magazine.

More on revision in the next chapter.

MORE EXERCISES FOR ENDINGS

1. Choose an anthology of short stories. Read the last paragraphs of the first four stories. Out of context, do they seem evocative, emotional, significant? Now read the four stories. In context, do the final paragraphs imply more than they seemed to at first?

2. Classify each of the four stories as "traditional plotted story" or "contemporary literary short story." Do the stories fit neatly into categories, or not? How do the endings of the two types differ?

3. Study each story's opening and closing paragraphs. Are any of the same symbols, motifs, or images present in both? If so, how has their meaning expanded or changed by the end of the story?

4. Study the final paragraphs of three of your favorite novels. Do they seem to carry thematic significance, or do they merely round off the action? Do you see any differences in the closing paragraphs of the novels from the closing paragraphs of the four short stories you examined in exercises one through three?

5. Look at the last paragraph of one of your own finished stories. Does it imply as much as it could? Even if the answer is *yes*, write three or four different last sentences for your story. Which works best? Why?

CHAPTER 9
HELP FOR ENDINGS:
THE LAST HURRAH

You've done it. There it is, sitting on the table in a pristine pile of pages. A first draft. It's finished. After weeks (or months or years), it's finally finished, with a beginning, a middle, and an end. You want to break out a bottle of champagne or turn a cartwheel or imagine—word for word—the review in the *Times*. It's actually *finished*. Go ahead, indulge. You've earned it. But when the bottle's empty or the reverie complete, come back down to earth and pick up those pages again. You're not finished yet.

As thousands of commencement speakers tirelessly remind us every June, it's in the nature of endings that they turn into new beginnings. Nowhere is this more true than in writing, where the term "first draft" automatically implies more to come. That "more" consists of the second and third (and maybe more) drafts.

Many new writers don't like to rewrite. After weeks—or months or years—of work on a story or novel, they want to consider it done. Yet revision is the single most important thing you can do for your work. In almost all cases, you'll end up with a much stronger story—and much better chances of selling it.

But how do you go about revision? If you knew a better way to write your tale, you'd have done it that way the first time, right? Well, no, not really. During the actual process of writing you learned a lot about your characters, plot, and setting. An organized approach to revision allows you to use that new knowledge to sharpen some aspects of your story, excise others, add background and secondary variations. You have the melody; revision can create the harmony.

There are as many ways to rewrite as there are writers. What follows is one organized approach. Try it, selecting whichever parts of the plan seem applicable to your particular work. This approach has six steps: (1) becoming the reader, (2) tracing the promise, (3) scene analysis, (4) major rewrite, (5) image patterns, and (6) polishing the prose.

STEP ONE: BECOMING THE READER

Although you may have revised sections of your story as you wrote them (the beginning scene, for instance), this is your first chance to consider the strengths and weaknesses of your manuscript as a whole. The first step in doing this is to not do it immediately. Put the story away for a while—a few days or a week or a month, depending on how long you need to get some distance from it. When you no longer think it is (a) absolutely brilliant, or (b) absolutely stupid (different writers have different postpartum reactions), you're ready to try to consider the manuscript dispassionately.

I say "try to" because you will never be able to be completely objective about your own work. No one can—this is your mind, your heart, your imagination set down in black and white. Still, a cooling-off period increases your chances of reading your story not as its writer, but as one of its future readers.

"Becoming the reader is the essence of becoming a writer," said author John O'Hara. Read over your short story or novel as if you've never seen it before. Jot quick notes in the margin: Where does the story seem to drag (you know it's dragging if your attention wanders while you're reading it)? What might be unclear if you didn't know the ending (and you *don't* if you're a reader picking up the story for the first time)? Your protagonist developed as you wrote her; does she seem sketchy in the first scenes, just one more generic office worker or housewife or private detective? Write "char, sketchy" in the margin. Do any scenes seem to go by too quickly? Are there places where you're telling us about important action, instead of dramatizing it for us? Write "dramatize!" in the margin. In fact, write *anything* in the margin that comes to you as you read. What would you think about this story if you'd never seen it before?

Sometimes it's useful to also have someone else read your story in this way. I say "sometimes" because, as you probably already know, not all friends or relatives are equally useful critics. Some will love anything you wrote just because you wrote it; others will attack anything you wrote for the same reason. Some won't care for your particular genre or won't understand its conventions. Some just can't verbalize reactions to fiction beyond "I liked it" or "I didn't like it." Some, on the other hand, will enthusiastically mark up every paragraph, in effect rewriting your story the way *they* would have written it.

But if you're fortunate to know someone who can and will tell you honestly which parts of the story are interesting and which are not, enlist this precious resource to read your first draft. He doesn't have to be able to tell you how to fix the problems; all you want at this stage is an informed, articulate aide—we'll call him "Sensitive Reader"—to help you spot trouble spots.

STEP TWO: TRACING THE PROMISE

You already worked on this step as you wrote. Now try to look with fresh eyes at the three parts of your story—beginning, middle, end—in terms of the implicit promise. You're still reading as a reader here, not a writer. Reread your first two pages, and then set the story down to think about them. What kind of experience do they seem to promise the reader?

Characters he can identify with? A glimpse into a different world? Thrills and excitement? An intellectual puzzle to solve? Insights into human nature? People he will love to hate? Try to formulate a sentence or two that accurately describe what your story promises.

If you are fortunate enough to have enlisted Sensitive Reader, ask him to do the same thing: Stop after the first few pages and jot down how he expected the rest of the story to go. The goal here is not to see if he can predict your exact ending, but to get his thoughts on what sort of story he hoped to see unfold from your beginning.

Pick up your story again and read the middle. Does it seem to develop those forces promised at the beginning? Make a list of all the forces your middle develops. If, for example, your beginning promised a detective troubled by personal problems and challenged by a difficult case, does the middle make clear what those personal problems are? Does the case provide enough complications and difficulties so that it really is challenging? Finally, do these various forces—the detective's personal concerns, the difficulties of the case, the goals of the other characters—move into opposition with each other so that your middle promises an interesting confrontation at the climax?

What does Sensitive Reader say when you ask *him* these questions?

Now reread your ending. Again, try to pretend you haven't seen the story before. Does it fulfill the promise? Specifically, do the forces come into satisfying clash at the climax? Does the denouement, if there is one, account for everything that needs to be accounted for? Are the expectations raised in the beginning of the story satisfied by the time the reader reaches the end?

If the answer to all these questions is *yes*, you've fulfilled the implicit promise. But if it's *no*, you need to determine where the story went awry. If the ending delivers something different than was promised in the beginning, one or the other will need to be rewritten. Your major task here is to determine which one. It's possible that major replotting will be involved.

Suppose, for instance, that you started writing about Sam, Martha, and Jane from Jane's point of view. Your beginning encourages us to identify with Jane, the mother. You do that by allowing us free access to all of Jane's thoughts, by painting her as a caring mother concerned for her daughter, by showing Sam's neglect of his family as the reason Martha runs away. But then, halfway through your story, you realize that your plot is more complex than that. No one person is to blame. Instead Martha's troubles come from a congruence of problems: Sam's preoccupation with work, Jane's envy of her daughter's youth, the friends Martha has fallen in with, the American culture as a whole. In fact, at the end of your book, Martha is going to die of an overdose.

Is this change of direction on your part actually a problem?

Yes, it is. In the beginning you offered us the promise that we were going to see a story of straightforward mother love, which might or might not be enough to rescue an erring daughter. We the readers have settled in for a satisfying, vicarious dose of good-woman-doing-her-best. But the promise you've fulfilled is different: an unflinching look at the American family. Jane isn't someone we want to identify with after all; we're not going to feel good; this is all *harder* than you promised. Readers will feel cheated. Many won't finish your book. Editors may not even buy it, *not* because it's gritty and downbeat, but because you promised us simple and upbeat.

So what do you do? You can adjust the beginning, rewriting so that we see from the beginning that Jane, even though she's the point-of-view character, has severe enough problems of her own that we might do better to observe her than to identify with her. You can introduce enough distance between reader and character so that identification isn't automatic. Or, alternatively, you can let us know that even though we're meant to identify with Jane because we like her, she has doubts about herself that we ought to pay attention to. In short, you can promise that this story is not going to be easy, and if we're after straightforward adventure or heartwarming happy endings, we'd better go elsewhere.

On the other hand, you could change your ending. Maybe Jane confronts her own jealousy of Martha, realizes that she's almost made a terrible mistake, and gets to Martha in time to save her. This would justify our original positive feelings for Jane and would deliver the affirmative ending your beginning promised.

I've deliberately chosen a subtle example here to show how carefully you must consider the implicit promise. Other disjunctions between beginning, middle, and end are easier to see. If you've promised to scare us and nothing scary happens, that's a broken promise. If you've been building toward a major gun battle and it never happens, that's a broken promise. If you've set up a baffling murder and shown your detective investigating suspects for three hundred pages, and it turns out the real murderer is someone who wasn't even a character in the story, that's a broken promise. If you've shown us a virtuous character and it turns out she was the murderer but your story contained absolutely no clues to that effect anywhere, that's a broken promise. If you fail to have the forces of your middle collide at the climax, that's a broken promise.

Once you know what your beginning promised, what forces your middle developed, and what your ending delivered, you can make sure that all three match.

STEP THREE: SCENE ANALYSIS

Now switch metaphorical hats, from reader to editor. We're about to look at the way stories are written: in scenes. Here's a technique some writers find useful.

Make a list of every scene in your short story by location or major event. For a novel, try listing the scenes in each chapter or section as you revise it. A partial list might look like this:

Scene	Place	Event	Point of view
1	home	Jane & Sam fight	Jane
2	home	Jane talks to Martha	Jane
3	city	Martha catches Greyhound	Martha
4	street	Sam hit by bus	Sam
5	home	Jane on phone with her mom	Jane

When you've finished, look at your list of scenes. Are there any you can cut? Are there any you can combine? A scene should both advance the plot and deepen our understanding of character. If any of your scenes is doing only one of these things, consider changing it.

For instance, if the scene of Jane talking on the phone with her mother has as its only purpose to show us Jane's background, maybe you could combine it with a slightly later scene in which Martha calls home just before her bus leaves town, to gloat or reassure or accuse. (Martha herself isn't sure why she called.) One call comes in on call-waiting while Jane's taking the other one. You get double mileage out of the same scene.

If there are places where, in your initial reading, you (or Sensitive Reader) thought the story dragged a bit, maybe you can cut out those scenes entirely (it's often astonishing how much you can cut without losing the reader). If there are events in that scene you absolutely must have, maybe you can pick up the pace by shortening the scene. Or consider summarizing it in exposition, if it's really dragging, so that you can move onto more interesting events. Four pages of description of all the small towns, as seen by Martha from the Greyhound window, might become:

> Five Corners, North Java, Johnsonburg, Alexander—she'd never seen so many white clapboard churches and Grain & Feeds. Nor so many cabbages. They clotted the fields like giant green and purple turds. Even with windows closed their smell hung heavy in the bus, pungent and rotting. Martha was glad when the bus finally pulled into Batavia.

Look at your scene analysis in terms of your other notes on the story. Try to see which scenes will need major rewriting to fulfill your implicit promise, flesh out characters, or develop the forces that will collide at the climax.

STEP FOUR: MAJOR REWRITE

When you're finished reading and analyzing your story, you might feel overwhelmed by all your reactions and ideas. There are so *many*. Where do you start?

Start at the beginning. Try to revise in order, the beginning and then the middle and then the end, so that you retain control over how the various scenes will appear to a reader. Take as long as you need for each part. Go back to the beginning as often as you must. Consult your margin notes, and those of Sensitive Reader. Rewriting involves hundreds of decisions, some small and some large; make each one as best you can, keeping in mind that all changes should help move your story toward its climax.

You might feel yourself going stale on the story: a reluctance to work on it or even to think about it, or a feeling in the pit of your stomach that that seems to indicate that nothing you're doing is actually improving the work. If so, put it away for a few days. If you still feel stale, shelve it for yet a few more days. If you *still* feel stale, maybe the story's done. Read it once more. You don't, after all, want to be one of those writers who goes on tinkering with the same short story for ten years.

When you've made all the major changes in scenes, characters, and structure that you're going to make, take a deep breath. You're almost to the end.

STEP FIVE: IMAGE PATTERNS

I've left revisions on image patterns until *after* the major rewrite, because until the basic scenes of your story are in place, it's difficult to control how those scenes use imagery. But now you've got your story in its almost-final form. Put it away for a few more days, and then look at it again in terms of the images you use consistently throughout.

In the last chapter, for instance, we looked at Stephen Minot's use of coldness and warmth in his short story "Sausage and Beer." In the beginning, everything the protagonist mentions is cold. His Uncle Theodore, in the mental institution, fears the cold. By the end of the story, as the boy's understanding and bond with his father grows, the images shift to the warmth of the speakeasy. Minot's use of temperature patterns underlines his basic theme: the importance of human connections in a morally cold universe. It also illuminates a basic danger of imagery.

Image patterns must fit naturally into the action scenes of your story. If you wait until the end and then try to graft on some pattern that wasn't there just because symbols are "literary," your image patterns will feel artificial. A good use of image patterns contributes to the unity of beginning, middle, and end; an artificial use makes a story seem mechanical and stiff. Minot's patterns of cold and warmth work because extremes of temperature are natural to the setting, which is New England in January.

What you do in this stage of revision, then, is not "think up" some alien image you can graft onto your story, but rather look for something already present in one part of the story that you can strengthen in the other parts.

My fantasy story "The Price of Oranges," for example, uses the image of an orange throughout. Harry, a pensioner living in a rundown retirement hotel, has discovered a passage though time (it's in the back of his closet) to September 1937. Harry is concerned that his best friend, skinny Manny, doesn't eat enough. He brings him food, including oranges, that he purchases in 1937, where his small pension buys much more. The story is not primarily about oranges—Harry has much larger plans for his trip back in time—but oranges crop up throughout as a symbol of what Harry is trying to accomplish.

At the end of the story, after Harry has decided to give up going back to 1937 (story events convince him of this), he gives Manny another orange. This one is a perfect specimen of modern, out-of-season, state-of-the-art orange growing, artificial pesticides and all— and it costs Harry five times what a 1937 orange had. The orange becomes a symbol of both gains and losses made explicit in the rest of the story.

Must your story or novel make use of image patterns? No, of course not. Many works (especially commercial novels) don't use them at all. But if you decide to develop an image pattern, first read through your story to choose some prop (such as an orange), aspect of setting (like Minot's use of cold), or symbol from the larger culture (John Updike, for instance, uses images from the Christian Mass in his short story "Giving Blood"). Consider how the image is used in your story. Ask yourself if it could appear again earlier, or later, with a slightly different meaning.

You want to use a light hand here. The resulting image pattern should be both natural to your story and unobtrusive. It must add to the meaningfulness of the characters' actions, not substitute for it.

STEP SIX: POLISHING THE PROSE

We talked about credible prose at the beginning of this book, and I won't repeat all the elements that make up good prose. What I *will* do is urge you to go through your entire manuscript one last time—yes, even if it's a novel—this time reading not for plot or character development, but on a sentence-by-sentence level. Look for diction that isn't sharp enough and substitute a better word. Straighten out awkward or convoluted sentences. Double-check spelling and punctuation. Make sure that the character who is seventeen years old on page forty-five isn't sixteen years old on page two hundred, which is supposed to be eight months later.

Your main job on this final draft, however, is to cut excess words wherever you can. It's truly amazing how much wordiness can creep in during the revision process. It's also amazing how much stories are sharpened by keeping your prose free of padding. ("Lean! Lean!" I write on my students' manuscripts. "Is this pork chops?" one wrote back. But his story was improved by trimming the verbal fat.)

ANOTHER VIEW OF REVISION

I can't leave the vital subject of revision without adding a caveat: Some writers don't do it this way. In fact, some writers hardly do it at all.

I'm reluctant to say that, because it might be taken as endorsement of the view that revision is not necessary. It almost always is. This is especially true for new writers, who are still learning their craft. But the truth is that there are writers who revise very little. Usually, like Isaac Asimov, they cultivate a plain, straightforward style that comes so naturally it doesn't need much polishing. Usually, again like Asimov, they have the entire story plotted in their heads before they begin, so that midcourse direction changes don't require massive alterations to earlier scenes. Usually, as well, they are experienced writers, sure of both their subject matter and their story structure.

But sometimes even writers who ordinarily revise will receive a "gift story"—one that flows so easily and completely from the pen that it seems a gift from somewhere outside themselves. My story "Out of All Them Bright Stars" was like that. Such stories, which are usually short, seem to "write themselves" in a single sitting. If you are given one, and it truly seems to arrive so complete that you can't think of anything you should change, rejoice.

But don't count on it. These stories are exceptions.

TWO PROMISES FULFILLED

You've worked hard and faithfully, and your story or novel is finished. Congratulations—you've fulfilled two promises. The first is in the story itself, the implicit promise to the reader. The second, equally important, is to yourself. You said you were going to write a whole story or novel, giving it everything you've got, and you did. That's an achievement to be admired.

Now what?

Now you mail that story out and begin another one.

The best thing you can do for yourself, when your story is truly finished, is to forget about it. Continue to market it, of course, but transfer your creative attention to the next story.

Let *that* one become the center of your speculation, effort, and hopes—not the one in the mail. Maybe that first one will sell, maybe not. Either way, you're still growing as a writer, and the best way to do that is to concentrate on what you're writing now, today, this moment.

"Writing is making sense of life," says Nobel laureate Nadine Gordimer. Which is why each new story, no matter how many you've written before, is a new, unlimited promise—to yourself.

Begin.

STILL MORE EXERCISES FOR ENDINGS

1. Find a story you finished at least six months ago. Read it in the way suggested in the section called "Becoming the Reader." Jot your responses to the story in the margin. Try to react as a reader, not a writer.

2. Take the same story and analyze its implicit promise. Is that promise developed in the middle of the story? Is it fulfilled at the end? If you know a Sensitive Reader, ask him to read the story and comment.

3. Sticking with the same story, now list its scenes. Is it clear to you what each is supposed to accomplish? Can scenes be combined or cut?

4. Decide whether this story is worth revising. Do you still like the central idea, the characters, or the plot, enough to work on it more? If so, revise it according to your analyses in exercises one through three.

5. Even if you don't choose to revise this story, pull out the first full page. Go through this page meticulously, cutting *every* word you can without losing any information. Reword for greater tightness whenever you can. Be ruthless. Retype the result. Does it read better? How much shorter is the page?

6. Write another story.

7. Write another.

8. Write.

EXCLUSIVE
Q & A WITH NANCY KRESS

You've been writing for decades. Have you seen any shifts in the way novelists plot their stories in recent years? Have trend shifts affected plotting conventions?

> Plotting is a highly individual activity. If there are "trends" in plotting I am unaware of them, with one possible exception: Young Adult novels. The plots in YA have gotten edgier, more graphic, and darker in the last decade or so.

What message do you find yourself repeating over and over to writers?

> Two messages: First, write more. Getting good at this takes practice, just as in all the arts. Second, dramatize your scenes, rather than relying on exposition. Readers want to see, hear, feel, smell the action of your story, even if that action is just two people having a quiet conversation.

What's the worst kind of mistake that new writers, freelancers, or book authors can make?

> Oh, there are so many! One would be closing your mind to feedback and criticism. Defensiveness interferes with growth as a writer.

Do you have any advice for new writers on fostering a strong author/editor relationship?

> Listen carefully, consider suggestions even more carefully, and if you disagree, present your disagreements without getting upset (not always easy). Also, be as patient as you can in waiting to hear from editors, who have very busy schedules. Not, however, infinitely patient; sometimes you have to remind them that you and your work still exist.

Do you have any advice for new writers on building an audience?

> Only the timeless advice: Write fiction that people want to read. I don't really think that the mall signings, postcards mailed to libraries, etc., have much effect on the overall numbers.

What should writers keep in mind regarding trends in publishing?

> Electronic platforms—Kindle, iBook, etc.—are increasingly important. Hold on to those rights if you can. But no matter who gets the money, work to get your books onto those platforms.

What do you feel is the biggest accomplishment of your career?

> I don't think there is a single one. Some books have been more successful than others (notably *Beggars in Spain*), but as I write my books, I'm intensely involved in all of them. The process, not the results, have to be the reason a writer writes. Otherwise, creating a four-hundred-page novel is just too daunting a task.

You began writing somewhat by accident—as a hobby while caring for your small children at home. How did this beginning have an affect on how you developed as a writer and how your career developed?

> I don't think it had any particular effect—what matters is not how you begin, but how you go on.

Over the course of your career, which aspect of story have you struggled with most: beginnings, middles, or ends? Why?

> Middles. The beginning usually comes to me clearly and all at once. By the time I reach the end, I know what will happen (if I don't, the piece is in deep trouble) and I'm steamrollering along. But in the middle I'm sometimes uncertain what should happen next and am just trying to muddle through.

You've written while caring for your children and working full-time. You now write full time. What has each type of writing life taught you?

> Full time is better. However, it does take more discipline. Nobody structures your time except you.

What piece of advice have you received over the course of your career that has had the biggest impact on your success?

> It was advice from science fiction writer Gene Wolfe, who said about short stories: "Have two different things going on in a story and then at the end have the two things impact each other." I have done so ever since.

What's the one thing you can't live without in your writing life?

> Coffee. Without coffee, nothing gets written. Period.

In what way has your writing/publishing life changed in the past 5 years?

> Again, electronic versions of my work have increased in importance. But the writing part (as opposed to marketing) is pretty much the same: I write the stories I get interested in.

Which part of the career is hardest for most writers: the beginning, middle, or later when they're an established author? Which has been most challenging for you?

The beginning is the hardest emotionally, because everything one writes gets rejected. And rejected again. And yet again. Persistence is required. The rejection never goes away entirely, but when it's balanced by some success, it's easier to bear. Or maybe one just develops a tougher hide.

Which part of the career has been most fun and rewarding for you?

When a story is flying along, and I'm so into it that my "real" world goes away, it can feel magical. I cease to be, my desk and computer ceases to be, and I am my character in his world. Psychologists call this a "flow state," and it's better than publication, money, awards, fame.

What advice do you have for writers in each stage?

Persist. In all stages. Also, read a lot. It's from reading and living that the creative well is replenished.

INDEX

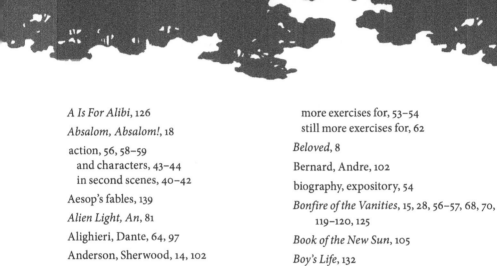

also dialogue
actions initiated by, 43–44
adding, 49–52
appearance of, 46–47, 54
body language of, 46
catalytic third, 52
and change, 42–43, 92–94, 97–98
developing, 42–47, 86–98
and endings, 114
example of, 22–24
gestures of, 46, 54
important, 67–68
introducing, 10–13, 42–47, 49–52
motivations of, 86–92
in openings, 10–13, 23–24
patterns of behavior in, 93–94
point-of-view, 45, 68–70, 74, 80–81
protagonists, 67–68, 146
reactions to other characters, 44
secondary, 49–52
thoughts of, 45, 56, 59–60, 62.
    See also point of view
villains, 95–97
Charley, 8–9
"Christmas Carol, A", 132, 136
"Cinderella", 132
    rewriting, 56–60, 72
"City of the Dead, A City of the Living,
    A", 96
Clan of the Cave Bear, 141
"Clean, Well-Lighted Place, A", 133–134,
    137, 140
clichés, avoiding, 18
climaxes
    dramatization of, 76–78
    and emotion, 118
    length of, 122
    of story, 66
    planning for, 76–78
    preparing for, 84, 113
    successful, 117–119, 129
closure, 123–124
Colwin, Laurie, 46–47
conflict, 7, 22, 26, 34, 54, 113

controlling, 37–38, 40
development of, 31–32, 91–92
and endings, 113
in openings, 13–15, 24
promise of, 52
in second scenes, 38–40
Connell, Richard, 65
Conrad, Joseph, 109–110
Cookie, 117
Corman, Avery, 35
craft, of writing, 2–3
credibility, 7, 22, 154
    in openings, 16–22, 25–26
Crichton, Michael, 29–30, 77, 122
criticism, ignoring, 158
Dann, Jack, 107
David Copperfield, 79–80
deadlines, creating, 102, 109–110
Death Committee, The, 82
Deliverance, 13
denouement, 122–125, 130, 135
    brevity in, 124–125
    dramatization in, 125
Denton, Bradley, 80–81
descriptions, 56–57, 59, 62
"Destructors, The", 14
details, specific, 15–16, 25–26, 62.
    See also specificity
deus ex machina, 118, 129
dialogue, 56–58, 62
    and characters, 44–45, 47–49, 54
Dickens, Charles, 109, 118, 132, 136
Dickey, James, 13
diction, 17–18
    checking, 154
Dillard, Annie, 109
Dispossessed, The, 82–83
Doyle, Arthur Conan, 132
dramatization, 158

science fiction, 29, 54, 97, 121

sentences
  awkward, 19–20
  construction of, 19–20, 25
  last, 28, 139–142
  variety in, 20–21, 25

series books, kinds of, 126–128

setting, 57

Seventh Heaven, 28–29

Sheckley, Robert, 101

Sherlock Holmes stories, 132

Sherwood, Valerie, 106

short stories
  climax in, 76–78
  conflict in, 91–92
  dramatization in, 90–91
  and endings, 131–143
  throughline in, 71
  types of, 132–138, 142

Snow Queen, The, 29

Something Happened, 109

Sontag, Susan, 8

Southey, Robert, 18

specificity, 7, 22, 31–32
  in openings, 15–16, 24–25

spelling, checking, 154

Starting Over, 141

Steel, Danielle, 15

Steinbeck, John, 13, 109

Stevenson, Robert Louis, 84

stories
  contemporary literary, 132–138
  kinds of, 132–138
  promise of, 7–10
  traditional plotted, 132, 135–136

Strange Case of Dr. Jekyll and Mr. Hyde, 85

structure, 78–84
  multiviewpoint chronological section, 81–82, 85
  parallel running scenes, 82–83
  regularly recurring viewpoints, 80–81

selection of, 83–85
straight chronological, 79–80

success, fear of, 100–102, 110

Swimming Pool Theory, 36

symbols, 113, 138–139, 142
  image patterns, 152–153
  words as, 1–2

systems, for writing, 108–111

thrillers, 54

throughlines, of stories, 67, 70–72, 84

"To Build a Fire", 52

To Kill A Mockingbird, 28

Tolstoy, Leo, 15, 142

Tolstoy Syndrome, 100–102

tone, 21–22, 31, 53

Trollope, Anthony, 109

Twain, Mark, 43, 122

Tyler, Anne, 15

Updike, John, 127–128, 153

Urban Renewal Theory of Writing Fiction, The, 31–32

Vinge, Joan D., 29

Violet Clay, 61

Wakefield, Dan, 141

War and Peace, 51

West, Jessamyn, 110

Wide Sargasso Sea, 85

Wolfe, Gene, 105, 160

Wolfe, Tom, 15, 56, 119–120

words. *See also* credibility
  correct usage of. See diction
  economy of, 18–19
  modifiers, excessive use of, 21
  parts of speech, 21
  as symbols. See symbols

World According to Garp, The, 126

Wouk, Herman, 96, 141

Writing Life, The, 109

wrong directions, 104–105

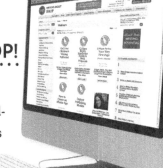